QUICK AND EASY
RECIPES
FOR YOUR
MICROWAVE

QUICK AND EASY RECIPES FOR YOUR MICROWAVE

by
Rena Croft

foulsham
LONDON . NEW YORK . TORONTO . SYDNEY

foulsham
Yeovil Road, Slough, Berkshire, SL1 4JH

ISBN   0-572-01943-2

Copyright © 1993 Strathearn Publishing. Ltd.

Printed in Great Britain by
Cox & Wyman Ltd,
Reading.

CONTENTS

INTRODUCTION

The microwave oven has become an essential tool in any well equipped kitchen. Microwave cooking is an efficient method of preparing food which preserves flavour and nutrients and saves time. What's more, the microwave oven can also be used to good advantage in conjunction with other appliances – the conventional oven, the grill (broiler), the freezer and the food processor.

It is fun to try out new recipes for the microwave, but what about all the old favourites? Everyone has recipes which are regularly enjoyed by family or friends, and the microwave can be used to cook those recipes – often saving time or making the job easier than ever. This book contains a varied selection of tasty everyday recipes specially adapted for the microwave so that you can make popular recipes quickly and easily.

Recipe Timing

One thing to remember when cooking in a microwave is that the timing for recipes can vary depending on the type of oven you are using, the exact quantities, how the foods have been prepared and how they are positioned in the microwave. On some dishes a minute or so too much can make a lot of difference. So the recipe times in the book have been indicated to take this into account. You will soon be able to judge timings to suit your own style of cooking. Always undercook rather than overcook foods; you can easily return them to the microwave for a few extra seconds or minutes, but you often cannot rescue them once overcooked. Remember, too, that some foods will continue to cook after they are removed from the microwave so bear this in mind when cooking.

Microwave Containers

There are a variety of containers which are suitable for microwave use: microwave plastic, pyrex and so on. Always use containers and utensils which are appropriate. If you use plastic film, use one which is designed for use in the microwave, not an ordinary cling film.

Experimentation

Once you have seen how to adapt some of your recipes to the microwave, you will soon find that experimenting on your own with other dishes becomes simple – and great fun. Apply similar principles to different types of fish, for example; use sauces for chicken with duck or turkey; or add different combinations of vegetables or different herbs and seasonings to casseroles or main courses. By experimenting, you will extend your range of dishes and become a real microwave expert.

NOTES FOR COOKS

- To reheat toast, place a slice on a sheet of kitchen paper and microwave on High for 15 seconds.
- To crisp up soft shelled nuts, microwave on High for 30 seconds to 1 minute.
- To loosen mousse from moulds, microwave on Low for 30 seconds.
- Heat a cup of milk on High for 1½-2 minutes.
- To make nuts easier to skin, place about 50 g/2 oz /½ cup of nuts in a dish and microwave on High for about 2 minutes, stirring once or twice during cooking. Leave to cool slightly then rub between your hands to remove the skins.
- To warm croissants, place them in the microwave with a glass of water and microwave on High for 30-45 seconds.
- Microwave oranges, lemons or other citrus fruits on High for 30 seconds each before squeezing and you will extract far more juice.
- To convert a conventional recipe to microwave cooking, reduce the cooking time to one quarter of the conventional time.
- Dishes require less water when cooked in the microwave. Reduce the quantity to one quarter of that used in a conventional recipe, especially when cooking casseroles.
- Make a note of how you prepare your own favourite recipes in the microwave so that you do not have to work it out twice.
- **All recipes are for 4 servings unless otherwise stated.**

Soups

AVOCADO SOUP

ingredients	Metric	Imperial	American
Chicken stock	600 ml	1 pt	2½ cups
Single (light) cream	120 ml	4 fl oz	½ cup
Ground cumin	2.5 ml	½ tsp	½ tsp
Salt and freshly ground black pepper			
Avocados, stoned, peeled and seeded	2	2	2
Lemon juice	15 ml	1 tbsp	1 tbsp
Small onion, chopped	1	1	1
Chopped fresh parsley	15 ml	1 tbsp	1 tbsp

method

1. Place the stock, half the cream and cumin in a casserole dish and season with salt and pepper. Microwave on High for 6-8 minutes until hot, stirring once or twice during cooking.

2. Place the avocados, lemon juice and onion in a food processor or blender and purée until smooth.

3. Stir the avocado mixture into the broth and pour it into a soup tureen. Swirl in the remaining cream to make a pattern then sprinkle with parsley.

BROCCOLI AND CAULIFLOWER SOUP

ingredients	Metric	Imperial	American
Broccoli florets, chopped	225 g	8 oz	½ lb
Cauliflower florets, chopped	225 g	8 oz	½ lb
Small onion, chopped	1	1	1
Potatoes, chopped	100 g	4 oz	¼ lb
Chicken stock	450 ml	¾ pt	2 cups
Single (light) cream	250 ml	8 fl oz	1 cup
Salt and freshly ground black pepper			
Chopped fresh chives	30 ml	2 tbsp	2 tbsp

method

1. Place the broccoli, cauliflower, onion, potatoes and stock in a large casserole dish. Cover and microwave on High for 16-20 minutes until the vegetables are tender, stirring twice during cooking.

2. Leave to stand for 4 minutes then purée in a food processor or blender, in batches if necessary.

3. Return the soup to the casserole and stir in the cream. Season to taste with salt and pepper. Microwave, uncovered, on High for 8-10 minutes until heated through, stirring twice during cooking.

4. Serve sprinkled with chives.

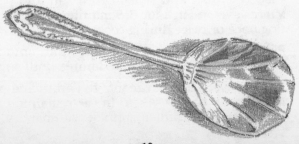

CARROT SOUP

ingredients	Metric	Imperial	American
Butter or margarine	75 g	3 oz	⅔ cup
Onion, chopped	1	1	1
Bacon rashers (slices), rinded and chopped	3	3	3
Pinch of sugar			
Salt and freshly ground black pepper			
Carrots, finely chopped	450 g	1 lb	1 lb
Chicken or vegetable stock	600 ml	1 pt	2½ cups
Toasted bread slice	1	1	1

method

1. Place the butter or margarine in a bowl and microwave on High for 1 minute until melted. Add the onion, bacon and sugar and season with salt and pepper. Microwave on High for 4 minutes.

2. Add the carrots and stock and microwave on High for 10 minutes until all the vegetables are tender, stirring once during cooking.

3. Purée the soup in a food processor or blender or rub it through a sieve.

4. Return the soup to the microwave and reheat on High for 2 minutes.

5. Cut the bread into cubes and serve the soup garnished with the croûtons.

CHICKEN AND VEGETABLE SOUP

ingredients	Metric	Imperial	American
Butter or margarine	30 ml	2 tbsp	2 tbsp
Carrot, chopped	1	1	1
Celery stalk, chopped	1	1	1
Onion, sliced	1	1	1
Chopped fresh parsley	15 ml	1 tbsp	1 tbsp
Garlic clove, crushed	1	1	1
Dried thyme	5 ml	1 tsp	1 tsp
Salt and freshly ground black pepper			
Plain (all-purpose) flour	45 ml	3 tbsp	3 tbsp
Mushrooms, sliced	100 g	4 oz	¼ lb
Cooked long-grain rice		100 g	4 oz ¼ lb
Chicken breasts, skinned and cut into strips	225 g	8 oz	½ lb
Chicken stock	450 ml	¾ pt	2 cups
White wine	45 ml	3 tbsp	3 tbsp
Milk	250 ml	8 fl oz	1 cup
Egg yolks	2	2	2

method

1. Put the butter or margarine, carrot, celery, onion, parsley, garlic and thyme in a bowl and season with salt and pepper. Cover and microwave on High for 6-7 minutes until the vegetables are tender, stirring occasionally during cooking.

2. Stir in the flour, mushrooms, rice, chicken, stock and wine. Cover and microwave on High for 8-10 minutes until thick, stirring occasionally during cooking.

3. Beat the milk and egg yolks together in a small bowl. Pour slowly into the soup, stirring continuously until blended.

4. Cover and microwave on Medium for 35 minutes until the chicken is cooked and the soup is hot, stirring once or twice during cooking.

CURRIED CHICKEN AND APPLE SOUP

ingredients	Metric	Imperial	American
Crisp eating apple, peeled, cored and chopped	1	1	1
Carrot, sliced	1	1	1
Celery stalk, sliced	1	1	1
Green pepper, chopped	½	½	½
Small onion, chopped	1	1	1
Oil	5 ml	1 tsp	1 tsp
Curry powder	5 ml	1 tsp	1 tsp
Pinch of grated lemon rind			
Pinch of ground cloves			
Salt and freshly ground black pepper			
Chicken stock	600 ml	1 pt	2½ cups
Canned chopped tomatoes	200 g	7 oz	7 oz
Chicken breast, cut into strips	225 g	8 oz	½ lb

method

1. Mix together the apple, carrot, celery, pepper, onion, oil, curry powder, lemon rind and clove and season with salt and pepper. Cover and microwave on High for 45 minutes until the vegetables are tender, stirring twice during cooking.

2. Add the remaining ingredients and mix well. Cover and microwave on High for 15-18 minutes until the chicken is cooked through, stirring several times during cooking.

13

VICHYSOISSE

ingredients	Metric	Imperial	American
Butter or margarine	50 g	2 oz	¼ cup
Leeks, thinly sliced	4	4	4
Chicken stock	375 ml	13 fl oz	1½ cups
Potatoes, cubed	2	2	2
Milk	375 ml	13 fl oz	1½ cups
Single (light) cream	120 ml	4 fl oz	½ cup
Sherry	45 ml	3 tbsp	3 tbsp
Salt and freshly ground black pepper			

method

1. Put the butter or margarine, leeks and 120ml/ 4 fl oz/¼ cup of stock in a bowl, cover and microwave on High for 8-10 minutes until the leeks are tender, stirring twice during cooking.

2. Put the potatoes and 75 ml/5 tbsp of broth in a bowl, cover and microwave on High for 6-8 minutes until tender, stirring once during cooking.

3. Pour the remaining stock and the potatoes into a food processor or blender and blend until smooth.

4. Stir the potato purée into the leeks with the milk and cream. Cover and microwave on Medium for 8-10 minutes until heated through, stirring twice during cooking. Stir in the sherry and season to taste with salt and pepper before serving hot or leave to cool and served chilled.

LENTIL SOUP

ingredients	Metric	Imperial	American
Onion, finely chopped	1	1	1
Garlic clove, crushed	1	1	1
Olive oil	15 ml	1 tbsp	1 tbsp
Dried lentils	225 g	8 oz	½ lb
Hot water	1.2 l	2 pts	5 cups
Carrots, thinly sliced	2	2	2
Celery stalk, finely chopped	1	1	1
Potato, diced	1	1	1
Canned passata (sieved tomatoes)	250 ml	8 fl oz	1 cup
Cooked ham, cubed	100 g	4 oz	¼ lb
Dried marjoram	5 ml	1 tsp	1 tsp
Salt and freshly ground black pepper			

method

1. Put the onion, garlic and olive oil in a bowl, cover and microwave on High for 2-3 minutes until tender.

2. Stir in the remaining ingredients except the salt and pepper. Cover and microwave on High for 5 minutes.

3. Stir well, then microwave on Medium for 45-50 minutes until the lentils are tender, stirring several times during cooking.

4. Season to taste with salt and pepper before serving.

MUSHROOM SOUP

ingredients	Metric	Imperial	American
Onion, sliced	1	1	1
Garlic cloves, chopped	2	2	2
Celery stalks, sliced	1	1	1
Oil	30 ml	2 tbsp	2 tbsp
Mushrooms, sliced	350 g	12 oz	¾ lb
Vegetable stock	600 ml	1 pt	2½ cups
Ground coriander	2.5 ml	½ tsp	½ tsp
Salt and freshly ground black pepper			
Single (light) cream	150 ml	¼ pt	⅔ cup

method

1. Put the onion, garlic, celery and oil in a bowl and microwave on High for 3-4 minutes until soft.

2. Add the mushrooms, stock and coriander and season with salt and pepper. Partially cover and microwave on High for 8-10 minutes, stirring once during cooking.

3. Purée the mixture in a food processor or blender. Return it to the microwave bowl and microwave on Medium for 2-3 minutes until heated through. Stir in the cream before serving

FRENCH ONION SOUP

ingredients	Metric	Imperial	American
Butter or margarine	100 g	4 oz	½ cup
Onions, thinly sliced	4	4	4
Garlic cloves, crushed	4	4	4
Brown sugar	5 ml	1 tsp	1 tsp
Vegetable stock	600 ml	1 pt	2½ cups
Grated nutmeg	2.5 ml	½ tsp	½ tsp
Salt and freshly ground black pepper			
French bread slices	6	6	6
Gruyère cheese, grated	100 g	4 oz	¼ lb

method

1. Put the butter or margarine, onions and garlic in a bowl and microwave on High for 3-4 minutes until soft. Stir in the sugar and microwave on High for 3 minutes.

2. Stir in the stock and nutmeg and season with salt and pepper. Microwave on High for 8-10 minutes.

3. Arrange the cheese on the bread slices. Put on a plate and microwave on High for 1 minute until melted. Serve the soup into bowls and place a bread slice in each bowl.

SPLIT PEA AND VEGETABLE SOUP

ingredients	Metric	Imperial	American
Split peas	175 g	6 oz	1 cup
Onion, chopped	1	1	1
Garlic clove, chopped	1	1	1
Dried oregano	5 ml	1 tsp	1 tsp
Vegetable stock	750 ml	1½ pts	3 cups
Salt and freshly ground black pepper			
Carrots, sliced	2	2	2
Celery stalks, sliced	2	2	2
Tomato purée (paste)	30 ml	2 tbsp	2 tbsp

method

1. Place the split peas, onion, garlic, oregano and stock in a large casserole dish and season with salt and pepper. Cover and microwave on High for 10 minutes.

2. Microwave on Medium for a further 20 minutes, stirring twice during cooking.

3. Add the carrots, celery and tomato purée, cover and microwave on Medium for 25 minutes until the vegetables are tender, stirring twice during cooking. Adjust the seasoning to taste before serving.

CREAM OF TOMATO SOUP

ingredients	Metric	Imperial	American
Butter or margarine	30 ml	2 tbsp	2 tbsp
Onion, chopped	1	1	1
Plain (all-purpose) flour	45 ml	3 tbsp	3 tbsp
Sugar	5 ml	1 tsp	1 tsp
Dried marjoram	5 ml	1 tsp	1 tsp
Salt and freshly ground black pepper			
Canned chopped tomatoes	400 g	14 oz	14 oz
Milk	450 ml	¾ pt	2 cups

method

1. Put the butter or margarine and onion in a bowl and microwave on High for 2 minutes.

2. Stir in the flour, sugar and marjoram and season with salt and pepper.

3. Purée the tomatoes in a food processor or blender. Stir into the casserole dish. Cover and microwave on High for 4-5 minutes until the soup thickens and bubbles, stirring occasionally during cooking.

4. Put the milk in a bowl and microwave on High for 2-3 minutes until hot. Whisk into the soup and microwave on High for 3-4 minutes until hot. Stir well.

WATERCRESS SOUP

ingredients	Metric	Imperial	American
Onion, sliced	1	1	1
Garlic cloves, crushed	2	2	2
Celery stalk, chopped	1	1	1
Potato, chopped	1	1	1
Oil	30 ml	2 tbsp	2 tbsp
Bunches of watercress	2	2	2
Vegetable stock	600 ml	1 pt	2½ cups
Grated nutmeg	2.5 ml	½ tsp	½ tsp
Salt and freshly ground black pepper			
Single (light) cream	45 ml	3 tbsp	3 tbsp

method

1. Put the onion, garlic, celery and potato in a bowl. Pour over the oil and microwave on High for 3-4 minutes.

2. Reserve a few watercress leaves for garnish. Remove the larger stalks and chop the remaining watercress. Add to the vegetables with the stock and season with nutmeg, salt and pepper. Partially cover and microwave on High for 8-10 minutes until the vegetables are tender, stirring once or twice during cooking.

3. Purée the soup in a food processor or blender then stir in the cream. Return to the microwave bowl and microwave on Medium for 2-3 minutes until heated through. Serve garnished with watercress.

ASPARAGUS WITH HOLLANDAISE SAUCE

ingredients	Metric	Imperial	American
Asparagus spears	450 g	1 lb	1 lb
Water	75 ml	5 tbsp	5 tbsp
Egg yolks, light beaten	2	2	2
Lemon juice	15 ml	1 tbsp	1 tbsp
Pinch of salt			
Pinch of cayenne pepper			
Butter or margarine	60 g	2½ oz	5 tbsp
Cucumber, peeled, seeded and finely chopped	¼	¼	¼
Chopped fresh dill (dill weed)	15 ml	1 tbsp	1 tbsp

method

1. Arrange the asparagus in a baking dish with the buds towards the centre. Add the water, cover with plastic wrap and microwave on High for 6-8 minutes until just tender, rearranging once during cooking. Drain and arrange on a warm serving plate. Cover and keep warm.

2. Mix together the egg yolks, lemon juice, salt and

cayenne in a food processor or blender until smooth.

3. Place the butter or margarine in a bowl and microwave on High for 1 minute until melted.

4. With the motor running on slow speed, gradually add the butter or margarine to the egg yolk mixture, blending until the sauce thickens.

5. Stir in the cucumber and dill, pour over the asparagus and serve at once.

MARINATED CORN

ingredients	Metric	Imperial	American
Corn cobs	4	4	4
Water	75 ml	5 tbsp	5 tbsp
Oil	120 ml	4 fl oz	½ cup
Orange juice	75 ml	5 tbsp	5 tbsp
Dijon mustard	15 ml	1 tbsp	1 tbsp
Honey	15 ml	1 tbsp	1 tbsp
Chopped fresh parsley	15 ml	1 tbsp	1 tbsp
Chopped fresh chives	15 ml	1 tbsp	1 tbsp
Chopped fresh dill (dill weed)	15 ml	1 tbsp	1 tbsp
Salt and freshly ground black pepper			

method

1. Arrange the corn cobs in a baking dish and pour over the water. Cover and microwave on High for 8-12 minutes until the corn is tender, rearranging twice during cooking. Drain and leave to stand for 4 minutes.

2. Mix together the remaining ingredients. Place the corn in a shallow dish and pour over the marinade. Turn the corn in the marinade, cover and chill for at least 4 hours before serving, turning the corn occasionally.

CRUDITES WITH VEGETABLE DIP

ingredients	Metric	Imperial	American
Carrot, finely chopped	1	1	1
Onion, finely chopped	1	1	1
Garlic clove, chopped	1	1	1
Red pepper, finely chopped	1	1	1
Butter or margarine	25 g	1 oz	2 tbsp
Water	15 ml	1 tbsp	1 tbsp
Cottage cheese	100 g	4 oz	1/2 cup
Plain yoghurt	75 ml	5 tbsp	5 tbsp
Lemon juice	15 ml	1 tbsp	1 tbsp
Cayenne pepper	2.5 ml	1/2 tsp	1/2 tsp
Salt and freshly ground black pepper			
For the crudités:			
Carrots	2	2	2
Celery stalks	2	2	2
Cucumber	1/2	1/2	1/2
Green pepper	1/2	1/2	1/2

method

1. Place the carrot, onion, garlic, pepper, butter or margarine and water in a casserole, cover and microwave on High for 3-4 minutes until the vegetables are tender but still crisp, stirring once during cooking.

2. Stir well and drain off any excess liquid.

3. Sieve the cottage cheese and mix with the remaining ingredients, seasoning to taste with salt and pepper. Stir in the drained vegetables, cover and chill.

4. Slice the vegetables into julienne strips and

arrange in an attractive pattern on a serving plate.
Serve with the dip.

Variation

You can use whatever fresh vegetables you prefer for the crudités.

STUFFED MUSHROOMS

ingredients	Metric	Imperial	American
Large mushrooms	8	8	8
Butter or margarine	25 g	1 oz	2 tbsp
Sherry	15 ml	1 tbsp	1 tbsp
Salt and freshly ground black pepper			
Camembert cheese, sliced	100 g	4 oz	¼ lb
Fresh parsley sprigs	8	8	8

method

1   Remove and chop the mushroom stems. Arrange the caps in a baking dish, stem side up.

2   Put the chopped stems, butter or margarine and sherry into a dish and microwave on High for 1-2 minutes until tender. Season with salt and pepper then spoon the mixture into the mushroom caps, pressing down gently. Arrange the cheese slices on top.

3   Microwave on Medium for 5-6 minutes until the cheese melts, rearranging the mushrooms once during cooking. Leave to stand for 5 minutes then garnish with parsley before serving.

HUMMUS

ingredients	Metric	Imperial	American
Lemon juice	75 ml	5 tbsp	5 tbsp
Water	90 ml	6 tbsp	6 tbsp
Sesame seeds	30 ml	2 tbsp	2 tbsp
Oil	5 ml	1 tsp	1 tsp
Onion, finely chopped	1	1	1
Garlic clove, finely chopped	1	1	1
Canned chick peas (garbanzo beans), drained	400 g	14 oz	14 oz
Chopped fresh parsley	30 ml	2 tbsp	2 tbsp

method

1. Place 15 ml/1 tbsp of lemon juice, 15 ml/1 tbsp of water, the sesame seeds and oil in a food processor or blender and process until smooth.

2. Pour the mixture into a casserole dish and add the remaining lemon juice and water, the onion and garlic. Cover and microwave on High for 4-5 minutes until the onion is soft.

3. Return the mixture to the processor, add the chick peas and process until smooth. Cover and chill before serving sprinkled with parsley.

CHICKEN LIVER PATE

ingredients	Metric	Imperial	American
Onion, finely chopped	1	1	1
Garlic clove, crushed	1	1	1
Butter or margarine	50 g	2 oz	¼ cup
Chicken livers, chopped	225 g	8 oz	½ lb
Brandy	15 ml	1 tbsp	1 tbsp
Salt and freshly ground black pepper			
Pinch of grated nutmeg			
Bay leave	2	2	2

method

1. Put the onion, garlic and butter or margarine in a bowl and microwave on High for 3-4 minutes until soft.

2. Stir in the chicken livers, cover and microwave on High for 3-5 minutes, stirring occasionally during cooking. Leave to cool slightly.

3. Purée the mixture in a food processor or blender with the brandy, salt, pepper and nutmeg.

4. Spoon the mixture into a serving dish, smooth the top and garnish with the bay leaves. Chill thoroughly before serving.

SMOKED HADDOCK PATE

ingredients	Metric	Imperial	American
Smoked haddock fillets	225 g	8 oz	½ lb
Milk	300 ml	½ pt	1¼ cups
Butter or margarine	75 g	3 oz	⅓ cup
Plain (all –purpose) flour	30 ml	2 tbsp	2 tbsp
Single (light) cream	45 ml	3 tbsp	3 tbsp
Dry sherry	15 ml	1 tbsp	1 tbsp
Salt and freshly ground black pepper			
Cucumber slices			

method

1. Place the haddock in a dish with 30 ml/2 tbsp of milk, cover and microwave on High for 4-5 minutes.

2. Drain the fish, reserving the liquid. Skin the fish and flake the flesh.

3. Place one-third of the butter or margarine in a bowl and microwave on High for 45 seconds. Stir in the flour until well blended. Whisk in the cooking liquor from the fish and the remaining milk. Microwave on High for 4 minutes, whisking 3 times during cooking.

4. Place the sauce and fish in a food processor or blender with the cream and sherry and process until smooth. Season to taste with salt and pepper. Transfer to individual dishes and chill. Garnish with cucumber slices and serve with buttered toast.

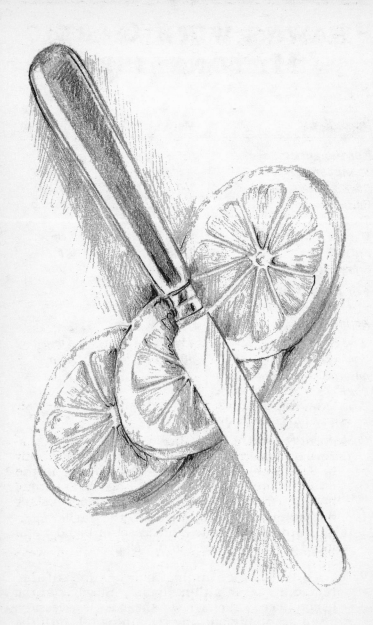

PRAWNS WITH GARLIC MAYONNAISE

ingredients	Metric	Imperial	American
For the garlic mayonnaise:			
Olive oil	300 ml	½ pt	1¼ cups
Garlic cloves	2	2	2
Egg	1	1	1
Mustard powder	5 ml	1 tsp	1 tsp
Salt	2.5 ml	½ tsp	½ tsp
Lemon juice	45 ml	3 tbsp	3 tbsp
For the prawns (shrimps):			
Garlic cloves, quartered	2	2	2
Olive oil	45 ml	3 tbsp	3 tbsp
Lemon juice	10 ml	2 tsp	2 tsp
Bay leaf	1	1	1
Pinch of salt			
Pinch of dried thyme			
Freshly ground black pepper			
Cooked peeled prawns (shrimps)	225 g	8 oz	½ lb

method

1. Put 30 ml/2 tbsp of olive oil, the garlic, egg, mustard and salt into a processor or blender and blend at medium speed until well mixed.

2. With the motor running, slowly add half the remaining oil in a thin stream. Slowly add the lemon juice, scraping down the sides if necessary. Then gradually add the remaining oil until the mixture is thick and smooth. Refrigerate for several hours to blend the flavours.

3. Put the ingredients for the prawn mixture, but not the prawns, in a bowl, cover and microwave on Medium for 3-5 minutes until the garlic is golden, stirring once during cooking.

4. Remove the garlic and stir in the prawns. Cover and microwave on medium for 2-4 minutes until the prawns are opaque, stirring once during cooking. Leave to stand, covered, for 2 minutes.

5. Remove the bay leaf and serve with the garlic mayonnaise.

PRAWN KEBABS

ingredients	Metric	Imperial	American
Cooked peeled large prawns (shrimps)	450 g	1 lb	1 lb
Spring onions (scallions)	7	7	7
For the marinade:			
Dry white wine	75 ml	5 tbsp	5 tbsp
Soy sauce	30 ml	2 tbsp	2 tbsp
Tomato ketchup (catsup)	15 ml	1 tbsp	1 tbsp
Sugar	5 ml	1 tsp	1 tsp
Sesame oil	2.5 ml	½ tsp	½ tsp
Chilli powder	2.5 ml	½ tsp	½ tsp

method

1. Put all the marinade ingredients into a bowl and microwave on High for 1 minute until very hot but not boiling. Stir well then leave to cool slightly. Stir in the prawns and leave to cool. Cover and chill for 3-4 hours.

2. Cut the spring onion into 2.5 cm/1 in pieces. Thread the spring onions and prawns alternately on to wooden skewers.

3. Arrange the skewers on a roasting rack, cover with greaseproof paper and microwave on Medium for 2-3 minutes until the prawns are opaque, turning them over once. Leave to stand for 1 minute before serving.

HOT PRAWN DIP

ingredients	Metric	Imperial	American
Celery stalk, chopped	1	1	1
Spring onions, sliced	2	2	2
Garlic clove, crushed	1	1	1
Butter or margarine	15 ml	1 tbsp	1 tbsp
Ground cumin	2.5 ml	½ tsp	½ tsp
Cream cheese	75 g	3 oz	3 oz
Natural yoghurt	120 ml	4 fl oz	½ cup
Tomato ketchup	15 ml	1 tbsp	1 tbsp
Cooked peeled prawns (shrimps)	100 g	4 oz	¼ lb
Seafood sticks, chopped	100 g	4 oz	¼ lb
Cheddar cheese, grated	50 g	2 oz	½ cup
Breadsticks			

method

1. Put the celery, onion, garlic, butter or margarine and cumin in a dish, cover and microwave on High for 2-3 minutes until tender. Set aside.

2. Put the cream cheese in a small bowl and microwave on Medium for 30-45 seconds until softened. Stir into the vegetable mixture.

3. Blend in the yoghurt and ketchup. Stir in the prawns and seafood sticks and mix well.

4. Sprinkle with cheese and microwave on Medium for 4-5 minutes until the cheese melts and the dip is hot. Leave to stand for 5 minutes.

5. Serve with breadsticks.

SPICY PRAWNS

ingredients	Metric	Imperial	American
Cooked peeled prawns (shrimps)	225 g	8 oz	8 oz
For the marinade:			
Beer	120 ml	4 fl oz	½ cup
Small onion, sliced	1	1	1
Grapefruit juice	15 ml	1 tbsp	1 tbsp
Mixed pickling spices	5 ml	1 tsp	1 tsp
Pinch of caraway seed			
Pinch of cayenne pepper			
Bay leaf	1	1	1
For the sauce:			
Chilli sauce	120 ml	4 fl oz	½ cup
Celery stalk, finely chopped	1	1	1
Grapefruit juice	10 ml	2 tsp	2 tsp
Grated onion	5 ml	1 tsp	1 tsp
Sugar	5 ml	1 tsp	1 tsp
Horseradish sauce	2.5 ml	½ tsp	½ tsp
Few drops of Worcestershire sauce			
Pinch of cayenne pepper			

method

1. Put all the marinade ingredients into a bowl and microwave on High for 2 minutes until boiling. Leave to cool slightly. Stir in the prawns and leave to cool.

2. Mix together all the sauce ingredients and chill.

3. Lift the prawns from the marinade, arrange on a roasting rack and cover with greaseproof paper. Microwave on Medium for 2-4 minutes until the prawns are opaque, turning once. Leave to cool then chill for 1 hour.

4. Arrange the prawns on crushed ice and serve with the spicy sauce.

SPICY CHICKEN BITES

ingredients	Metric	Imperial	American
Boned chicken breast	350 g	12 oz	¾ lb
Light soy sauce	90 ml	6 tbsp	6 tbsp
Oil	15 ml	1 tbsp	1 tbsp
Grated rind and juice of orange	1	1	1
Grated ginger root	5 ml	1 tsp	1 tsp
Ground cinnamon	2.5 ml	½ tsp	½ tsp
Freshly ground black pepper			
Broccoli florets	225 g	8 oz	½ lb

method

1. Place the chicken breasts between 2 sheets of plastic wrap and flatten them with a steak mallet or rolling pin. Cut into 5 cm/2 in squares and place in a bowl.

2. Mix together all the remaining ingredients except the broccoli, pour over the chicken, cover and chill for at least 2 hours.

3. Drain the chicken and discard the marinade.

4. Arrange the chicken pieces in a single layer in a casserole dish. Cut the broccoli into small florets and place one on top of each chicken piece. Cover and microwave on High for 5-7 minutes until the chicken is cooked through and the broccoli is just tender, rearranging once during cooking.

MEATBALLS WITH SWEET AND SOUR SAUCE

ingredients	Metric	Imperial	American
Minced (ground) beef	450 g	1 lb	1 lb
Dried breadcrumbs	75 g	3 oz	1/3 cup
Garlic clove, chopped	1	1	1
Grated ginger root, chopped	5 ml	1 tsp	1 tsp
Mustard powder	2.5 ml	1/2 tsp	1/2 tsp
Salt and freshly ground black pepper			
Tomato ketchup (catsup)	150 ml	1/4 pt	2/3 cup
Honey	100 ml	3 1/2 fl oz	6 1/2 tbsp
Soy sauce	75 ml	5 tbsp	5 tbsp

method

1. Mix together the beef, breadcrumbs, garlic, ginger and mustard and season with salt and pepper. Shape into small meatballs and arrange in a large casserole dish. Cover and microwave on High for 6-8 minutes until firm and browned, rearranging twice during cooking. Drain off any excess fat.

2. Mix together the tomato ketchup, honey and soy sauce and pour over the meatballs. Stir, cover and microwave on High for 2-4 minutes until hot, stirring gently twice during cooking.

ITALIAN PASTA SALAD

ingredients	Metric	Imperial	American
Boneless chicken brest, skinned	1	1	1
Cooked pasta	225 g	8 oz	½ lb
chopped tomatoes	225 g	8 oz	½ lb
Canned artichoke hearts, drained and sliced	100 g	4 oz	¼ lb
Black olives, sliced	6	6	6
Feta cheese, crumbled	100 g	4 oz	¼ lb
Chopped fresh parsley	45 ml	3 tbsp	3tbsp
Onion, chopped	1	1	1
Olive oil	120 ml	4 fl oz	½ cup
Lemon juice	45 ml	3 tbsp	3 tbsp
Dried oregano	5 ml	1 tsp	1 tsp
Salt	2,5 ml	½ tsp	½ tsp

method

1. Place the chicken on a microwave rack and microwave on High for 4-5 minutes until meat is no longer pink and the juices run clear, turning over once during cooking. Leave to stand, covered, for 3 minutes. Slice into strips.

2. In a large mixing bowl, combine the chicken with the pasta, tomatoes, artichoke hearts, olives, cheese, parsley and onion.

3. In a separate bowl, whisk together the olive oil, lemon juice, oregano and salt. Pour over the salad, cover and leave to marinate for 4 hours until cold.

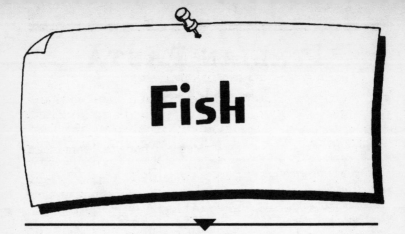

COD IN LEMON-PINEAPPLE SAUCE

ingredients	Metric	Imperial	American
Cod fillets, cut into serving pieces	450 g	1 lb	1 lb
Butter or margarine	15 ml	1 tbsp	1 tbsp
Lemon juice	15 ml	1 tbsp	1 tbsp
Garlic clove, crushed (optional)	1	1	1
Salt and freshly ground black pepper			
For the sauce:			
Soft brown sugar	30 ml	2 tbsp	2 tbsp
Cornflour (cornstarch)	15 ml	1 tbsp	1 tbsp
Chicken stock	120 ml	4 fl oz	½ cup
Lemon juice	30 ml	2 tbsp	2 tbsp
Tomato purée (paste)	15 ml	1 tbsp	1 tbsp
White wine vinegar	15 ml	1 tbsp	1 tbsp
Canned pineapple chunks, drained	225 g	8 oz	½ lb

method

1. Arrange the fish in a baking dish.

2. Place the butter or margarine in a small bowl and microwave on High for 45 seconds until melted. Stir in the lemon juice. Brush over the fish, sprinkle with the garlic, if using, and season with salt and pepper.

3. Cover and microwave on High for 4-6 minutes until the fish flakes when tested with a fork, rearranging the fish once during cooking.

4. Mix together all the sauce ingredients except the pineapple. Microwave on High for 5-6 minutes until thick, stirring once during cooking. Stir in the pineapple and microwave on Medium for 2 minutes until heated through.

5. Arrange the fish on a warmed serving plate, pour over the sauce and serve with rice.

COD IN SOURED CREAM SAUCE

ingredients	Metric	Imperial	American
Butter or margarine	45 ml	3 tbsp	3 tbsp
Plain (all-purpose) flour	25 g	1 oz	1/4 cup
Pinch of grated nutmeg			
Salt and freshly ground black pepper			
Milk	250 ml	8 fl oz	1 cup
Soured cream	60 ml	4 tbsp	4 tbsp
Cod fillets, cubed	450 g	1 lb	1 lb
Paprika			

method

1. Put 30 ml/2 tbsp of butter in a bowl and microwave on High for 45 seconds until melted.

2. Stir in the flour and nutmeg and season with salt and pepper. Blend in the milk. Microwave on High for 3-4 minutes until the mixture thickens and bubbles, stirring once or twice during cooking. Stir in the soured cream.

3. Place the cod in a casserole dish and dot with the remaining butter. Cover and microwave on High for 4-6 minutes until the fish flakes easily with a fork, stirring once during cooking. Drain any excess liquid.

4. Pour the sauce over the cod then microwave on Medium for 2 minutes until heated through.

5. Serve sprinkled with paprika.

FISH PIE

ingredients	Metric	Imperial	American
Cod fillets, skinned	450 g	1 lb	1 lb
Butter or margarine	50 g	2 oz	¼ cup
Plain (all-purpose) flour	25 g	1 oz	¼ cup
Milk	300 ml	½ pt	1¼ cups
Salt and freshly ground black pepper			
Tomato purée (paste)	15 ml	1 tbsp	1 tbsp
Hard-boiled (hard-cooked) egg, chopped	1	1	1
Cooked peeled prawns (shrimps)	100 g	4 oz	¼ lb
Mashed potatoes	350 g	12 oz	¾ lb
Tomato, sliced	1	1	1

method

1. Place the fish on a plate, cover and microwave on High for 3 minutes until it flakes easily when tested with a fork. Flake the fish into a bowl.

2. Place half the butter or margarine in a measuring jug and microwave on High for 45 seconds until melted. Stir in the flour then blend in the milk and season with salt and pepper. Microwave on High for 2-3 minutes until thick, stirring occasionally during cooking.

3. Stir the tomato purée into the sauce. Gently fold the fish, hard-boiled egg and prawns into the sauce. Check and adjust the seasoning to taste.

4. Spoon the mixture into a baking dish and cover with the potatoes. Dot with the remaining butter and microwave on High for 5 minutes until heated through. Serve garnished with tomato.

HADDOCK IN BREADCRUMBS

ingredients	Metric	Imperial	American
Butter or margarine	50 g	2 oz	¼ cup
Garlic clove	1	1	1
Dried breadcrumbs	75 g	3 oz	¾ cup
Parmesan cheese, grated	25 g	1 oz	¼ cup
Chopped fresh basil	5 ml	1 tsp	1 tsp
Salt and freshly ground black pepper			
Haddock fillets, cut into chunks	450 g	1 lb	1 lb
Chopped fresh parsley	30 ml	2 tbsp	2 tbsp

method

1. Put the butter or margarine ánd garlic into a baking dish and microwave on High for 1-2 minutes until the butter melts.

2. In a shallow dish, mix together the breadcrumbs, cheese and basil and season with salt and pepper.

3. Place the haddock pieces in the melted butter and stir to coat. Roll them in the breadcrumb mixture, pressing lightly to coat on all sides.

4. Arrange the haddock on a roasting rack and microwave on High for 6-8 minutes until the fish flakes easily with a fork , rearranging the fish once during cooking.

5. Serve garnished with parsley.

BAKED MACKEREL

ingredients	Metric	Imperial	American
Mackerel	4	4	4
Onion, thinly sliced	1	1	1
White wine vinegar	150 ml	¼ pt	⅔ cup
Water	150 ml	¼ pt	⅔ cup
Salt and freshly ground black pepper			
Bay leaves	2	2	2
Lemon, cut into wedges	1	1	1

method

1. Clean the mackerel and remove the backbone.

2. Arrange the onion in a shallow baking dish. Pour over the wine vinegar and water and season with salt and pepper. Lay the bay leaves on top.

3. Place 2 mackerel on top and microwave on High for 8-9 minutes until the fish flakes easily when tested with a fork, turning the fish twice during cooking.

4. Transfer the fish to a serving plate and keep it warm. Add the other 2 fish to the liquid and microwave for 8-9 minutes until tender. Transfer to the serving plate and garnish with a few of the onion rings.

5. Leave the fish to cool and serve cold with salad garnish with lemon wedges.

PLAICE WITH CHEESE TOPPING

ingredients	Metric	Imperial	American
Butter or margarine	25 g	1 oz	2 tbsp
Plaice fillets	450 g	1 lb	1 lb
Salt and freshly ground black pepper			
Onion, chopped	1	1	1
Garlic clove, crushed	1	1	1
Tomatoes, skinned and chopped	2	2	2
Chopped fresh parsley	45 ml	3 tbsp	3 tbsp
Cheddar cheese, grated	50 g	2 oz	½ cup

method

1. Put the butter or margarine into a casserole dish and microwave on High for 45 seconds until melted.

2. Add the plaice and stir gently to coat the fish in the butter. Sprinkle with salt and pepper on both sides then sprinkle with the onion, garlic, tomatoes and 30 ml/2 tbsp of parsley. Cover and microwave on Medium for 8-10 minutes until the fish flakes easily with a fork, rearranging the fish once or twice during cooking.

3. Sprinkle the cheese over the fish, cover and microwave on High for 1 minute until the cheese melts. Leave to stand, covered, for 2 minutes before serving sprinkled with the remaining parsley.

Crab and Mushroom Gratin

ingredients	Metric	Imperial	American
Butter or margarine	30ml	2tbsp	2 tbsp
Spring onions, chopped	2	2	2
Plain flour	30ml	2tbsp	2 tbsp
Salt and freshly ground black pepper			
Pinch of cayenne pepper			
Whipping (heavy) cream	250 ml	8 fl oz	1 cup
White wine	15 ml	1tbsp	1tbsp
Button mushrooms	50 g	2 oz	2 oz
Crab meat, flaked	100 g	4 oz	1/4 lb
Parmesan cheese, grated	30 ml	2 tbsp	2 tbsp
Cheddar cheese, grated	100 g	4 oz	1/4 lb
Fresh parsley sprigs	2	2	2
Lemon, sliced	1/2	1/2	1/2

method

1. Put the butter or margarine and spring onion into a bowl and microwave on High for 45-60 seconds until the butter has melted.

2. Add the flour, salt, pepper and cayenne. Stir in the cream, wine and mushrooms. Microwave on medium for 4-5 minutes until thickened, stirring every minute during cooking.

3. Stir in crab meat and parmesan cheese. Divide the mixture between 4 ramekin dishes and sprinkle with the cheddar. Microwave on Medium for 3-5 minutes until the cheese melts.

4. Serve garnished with parsley and lemon slices.

SALMON WITH DILL SAUCE

ingredients	Metric	Imperial	American
For the sauce:			
Soured cream	120 ml	4 fl oz	½ cup
Milk	15 ml	1 tbsp	1 tbsp
Chopped fresh dill (dill weed)	5 ml	1 tsp	1 tsp
For the fish and vegetables:			
Carrots, thickly sliced	2	2	2
Courgettes (zucchini), thickly sliced	2	2	2
Vegetable stock	450 ml	¾ pt	2 cups
Salmon steaks	4	4	4
Salt and freshly ground black pepper			
Chopped fresh dill (dill weed)	15 ml	1 tbsp	1 tbsp

method

1. Mix together the sauce ingredients and chill for at least 1 hour.

2. Place the carrots and courgettes in a bowl and pour over the stock. Cover and microwave on High for 8-9 minutes until boiling, stirring once during cooking. Microwave on Medium for a further 4 minutes until the vegetables are just tender but still crisp.

3. Arrange the salmon steaks in a single layer in a casserole dish with the thick parts to the outside. Cover and microwave on Medium for 8-10 minutes until the salmon flakes when tested with a fork.

4. Spoon the vegetables and stock over the salmon and season with salt and pepper. Cover and

microwave on Medium for 2 minutes. Leave to stand, covered, for 5 minutes.

5. Lift the salmon from the casserole and arrange on a warm serving plate. Lift the vegetables from the stock with a slotted spoon and arrange around the salmon. Spoon a little of the stock over the top just to moisten the vegetables and sprinkle with dill. Serve with the chilled sauce.

SOLE WITH MUSTARD SAUCE

ingredients	Metric	Imperial	American
Butter or margarine	50 g	2 oz	¼ cup
Spring onions (scallions), thinly sliced	3	3	3
Sole fillets	450 g	1 lb	1 lb
Button mushrooms, sliced	100 g	4 oz	¼ lb
Dry white wine	120 ml	4 fl oz	½ cup
Lemon juice	15 ml	1 tbsp	1 tbsp
Chopped fresh parsley	30 ml	2 tbsp	2 tbsp
Dijon mustard	10 ml	2 tsp	2 tsp
Salt and freshly ground black pepper			
Plain (all-purpose) flour	15 ml	1 tbsp	1 tbsp
Lemon, sliced	1	1	1

method

1. Put half the butter or margarine and the spring onions into a bowl and microwave on High for 1-2 minutes until the spring onions are tender.

2. Cut the sole into serving pieces and arrange in a casserole dish with the thickest parts to the outside. Spoon the spring onion mixture over the top and sprinkle with the mushrooms.

3. Mix together the wine, lemon juice, parsley and mustard and season with salt and pepper. Cover and microwave on High for 7-9 minutes until the fish flakes easily when tested with a fork, rearranging the pieces once during cooking.

4. Transfer the fish and vegetables to a warmed serving dish and keep it warm. Drain the cooking juices into a measuring jug, make up to 250 ml/ 8 fl oz/1 cup with water.

5. Put the remaining butter or margarine into a small bowl and microwave on High for 45 seconds until the butter melts. Stir in the flour and blend in the cooking liquid. Microwave on High for 1-1$\frac{1}{4}$ minutes until the mixture thickens and bubbles, stirring once during cooking.

6. Pour the sauce over the sole and serve garnished with lemon slices.

TROUT WITH WINE SAUCE

ingredients	Metric	Imperial	American
Trout	4	4	4
Salt and freshly ground black pepper			
Butter or margarine	25 g	1 oz	2 tbsp
Chopped fresh parsley	15 ml	1 tbsp	1 tbsp
Grated lemon rind	15 ml	1 tbsp	1 tbsp
Dry white wine	150 ml	¼ pt	⅔ cup
Cornflour (cornstarch)	5 ml	1 tsp	1 tsp
Capers	10 ml	2 tsp	2 tsp

method

1. Clean the trout and sprinkle the inside with salt and pepper.

2. Place the butter or margarine in a bowl and microwave on High for 30 seconds until melted. Brush over the outside of the fish. Mix together the parsley and lemon rind and sprinkle inside the fish.

3. Place 2 fish in a baking dish, pour over the wine, cover and microwave on High for 6-7 minutes until the fish is tender. Lift out the fish and arrange on a warm serving dish. Place the other 2 fish in the liquid, cover and microwave on High for 6-7 minutes. Transfer the fish to the serving dish.

4. Pour the cooking liquid into a bowl and blend in the cornflour. Microwave on High for 30 seconds until thickened, then stir well and pour over the fish. Serve sprinkled with capers.

TUNA-FILLED POTATOES

ingredients	Metric	Imperial	American
Baking potatoes	4	4	4
Butter or margarine	50 g	2 oz	¼ cup
Small onion, sliced	1	1	1
Celery stalk, chopped	1	1	1
Chopped fresh parsley	15 ml	1 tbsp	1 tbsp
Soured cream	45 ml	3 tbsp	3 tbsp
Single (light) cream or milk	30 ml	2 tbsp	2 tbsp
Chopped fresh chives	10 ml	2 tsp	2 tsp
Salt and pepper			
Canned tuna, drained	200 g	7 oz	7 oz
Cheddar cheese, grated	50 g	2 oz	½ cup

method

1. Prick the potatoes with a fork, arrange on kitchen paper and microwave on High for 12-16 minutes until tender, rearranging once during cooking. Wrap in foil and leave to stand for 10 minutes.

2. Put the butter or margarine, onion, celery and parsley in a bowl and microwave on High for 2-3 minutes until just tender, stirring once during cooking.

3. Slice the tops off the potatoes and scoop out the insides, leaving a 5 mm/¼ in shell. Arrange the shells on a plate lined with kitchen paper.

4. Mix the potato flesh into the vegetables then stir in the soured cream, single cream or milk and chives, and season with salt and pepper. Beat until smooth. Stir in the tuna and half the cheese.

5. Spoon the mixture back into the potato shells and sprinkle with the remaining cheese. Microwave on High for 4-5 minutes until heated through.

51

TOMATO PASTA WITH PRAWNS

ingredients	Metric	Imperial	American
Olive oil	45 ml	3 tbsp	3 tbsp
Small onion, chopped	1	1	1
Garlic clove, crushed	1	1	1
Mushrooms, sliced	100 g	4 oz	4 oz
Courgettes (zucchini), cubed	2	2	2
Chopped fresh parsley	30 ml	2 tbsp	2 tbsp
Dried basil	2.5 ml	½ tsp	½ tsp
Pinch of dried thyme			
Canned tomatoes	400 g	14 oz	14 oz
Canned passata (sieved tomatoes)	150 ml	¼ pt	⅔ cup
Sugar	5 ml	1 tsp	1 tsp
Salt and freshly ground black pepper			
Pasta shells	350 g	12 oz	¾ lb
Cooked peeled prawns (shrimps)	450 g	1 lb	1 lb

method

1. Put the oil, onion and garlic in a bowl and micro-wave on High for 1 minute.

2. Stir in the mushrooms, courgettes, parsley, basil and thyme and microwave on High for 2-3 minutes until the vegetables are tender.

3. Add the remaining ingredients except the prawns, cover and microwave on Medium for 10-15 minutes, stirring once during cooking.

4. Meanwhile, cook the pasta in boiling salted water on the conventional oven for about 10 minutes until tender. Drain well then return to the hot pan.

5. Stir the prawns into the sauce, cover and microwave on Medium for 2-3 minutes until the prawns are heated through, stirring once during cooking. Leave to stand, covered, for 2 minutes. Pour over the pasta and toss together well before serving.

PRAWN FRIED RICE

ingredients	Metric	Imperial	American
Vegetable oil	15 ml	1 tbsp	1 tbsp
Onion, chopped	1	1	1
Frozen mixed vegetables, thawed	225 g	8 oz	½ lb
Cooked brown rice	225 g	8 oz	1 cup
Soy sauce	30 ml	2 tbsp	2 tbsp
Cooked peeled prawns	350 g	12 oz	¾ lb
Eggs, beaten	4	4	4
Salt and freshly ground black pepper			

method

1. Place the oil and onion in a bowl, cover and microwave on High for 4 minutes, stirring once.

2. Add the vegetables and microwave on high for 2 minutes. Stir in the rice, soy sauce, prawns and microwave on High for 4 minutes.

3. Stir in the egg and microwave on High for 1-2 minutes until lightly set. Season with salt and pepper.

QUICK PRAWN CURRY

ingredients	Metric	Imperial	American
Butter or margarine	50 g	2 oz	1/4 cup
Onion, chopped	1	1	1
Eating apple, peeled, cored and chopped	1	1	1
Plain (all-purpose) flour	25 g	1 oz	1/4 cup
Curry powder	10 ml	2 tsp	2 tsp
Salt and freshly ground black pepper			
Lemon juice	2.5 ml	1/2 tsp	1/2 tsp
Chicken stock	450 ml	3/4 pt	2 cups
Cooked peeled prawns (shrimps)	450 g	1 lb	1 lb

method

1. Put the butter or margarine into a bowl and microwave on High for 45 seconds until melted. Add the onion and microwave on High for 3-4 minutes until soft, stirring once during cooking.

2. Add the apple and microwave for 1 minute.

3. Stir in the flour and curry powder and season with salt and pepper. Cover and microwave on High for 1 minute.

4. Stir in the lemon juice and stock, cover and microwave on High for 6-8 minutes, stirring occasionally during cooking.

5. Add the prawns and microwave on High for 3-4 minutes until heated through.

Poultry

CHICKEN WITH BUTTER SAUCE

ingredients	Metric	Imperial	American
Carrots, cut into julienne strips	225 g	8 oz	½ lb
Courgettes (zucchini), cut into julienne strips	225 g	8 oz	½ lb
Chicken breasts, boned and halved	4	4	4
Pinch of paprika			
Salt and freshly ground black pepper			
Chicken stock	120 ml	4 fl oz	½ cup
Chopped fresh parsley	15 ml	1 tbsp	1 tbsp
Butter or margarine	50 g	2 oz	¼ cup
Lemon juice	5 ml	1 tsp	1 tsp

method

1. Arrange the carrots and courgettes in the bottom of a casserole dish and top with the chicken. Sprinkle with paprika, salt and pepper.

2. Pour over the chicken stock and sprinkle with parsley. Cover with kitchen paper and microwave

on High for 5-7 minutes until the chicken is tender and cooked through, rearranging once during cooking. Leave to stand for 4 minutes.

3. Mix together the butter or margarine and lemon juice in a measuring jug and season to taste with salt and pepper. Microwave on High for 45 seconds until melted. Spoon over the chicken and vegetables before serving.

CHILLI CHICKEN WINGS

ingredients	Metric	Imperial	American
Small onion, grated	1	1	1
Garlic clove, crushed	1	1	1
Soy sauce	45 ml	3 tbsp	3 tbsp
water	30 ml	2 tbsp	2 tbsp
Lime juice	30 ml	2 tbsp	2 tbsp
Dark brown sugar	15 ml	1 tbsp	1 tbsp
Ground coriander	5 ml	1 tsp	1 tsp
Ground cumin	2.5 ml	½ tsp	½ tsp

method

1. Separate the chicken wings into 3 parts at the joints and discard the wing tips.

2. Put the remaining ingredients into a large plastic bag, add the chicken wings and shake to mix. Tie the bag securely and refrigerate overnight, turning the bag over once or twice.

3. Put the chicken and marinade into a casserole dish, cover and microwave on High for 11-13 minutes until the chicken is cooked through, stirring 2 or 3 times during cooking.

STUFFED CHICKEN BREASTS

ingredients	Metric	Imperial	American
Boneless chicken breasts, skinned	4	4	4
Butter or margarine	25 g	1 oz	1 tbsp
Mushrooms, sliced	50 g	2 oz	2 oz
Onion, finely chopped	1	1	1
Seedless grapes, sliced	100 g	4 oz	4 oz
Dried breadcrumbs	25 g	1 oz	¼ cup
Raisins	50 g	2 oz	⅔ cup
Pinch of ground coriander			
Salt and freshly ground black pepper			
Mushroom Sauce (see page 113)	300 ml	½ pt	1¼ cups
Chopped fresh parsley	30 ml	2 tbsp	2 tbsp

method

1. Pound the chicken breasts until 5 mm/¼ in thick.

2. Place the butter or margarine, mushrooms and onion in a bowl, cover and microwave on High for 2 minutes.

3. Stir in the grapes, breadcrumbs, raisins and coriander and season with salt and pepper.

4. Spread the stuffing mixture over the chicken breasts almost to the edges. Fold in the sides, roll up and secure with cocktail sticks (toothpicks). Arrange in a casserole dish seam-side down.

5. Pour the sauce over the chicken, cover and microwave on Medium for 16-25 minutes until the chicken is cooked through and tender, rearranging twice during cooking.

6. Leave to stand, covered for 5 minutes then remove the cocktail sticks (toothpicks) before serving.

HONEYED CHICKEN BREASTS

ingredients	Metric	Imperial	American
Chicken breasts, halved and skinned	4	4	4
Honey	30 ml	2 tbsp	2 tbsp
Lemon juice	15 ml	1 tbsp	1 tbsp
Soft brown sugar	15 ml	1 tbsp	1 tbsp
Soy sauce	15 ml	1 tbsp	1 tbsp
Chopped fresh parsley	15 ml	1 tbsp	1 tbsp
Pinch of grated lemon rind			

method

1. Score the chicken breasts diagonally using a sharp knife and arrange them in a dish.

2. Mix together the remaining ingredients until well blended. Pour over the chicken, cover and chill for 1 hour.

3. Arrange the chicken pieces on a roasting rack with the thickest portions to the outside. Brush with the marinade. Cover and microwave on High for 12-15 minutes until the chicken is cooked through, rearranging the chicken and basting several times with the marinade during cooking until the marinade is used up. Serve with a crisp salad.

MARINATED CHICKEN

ingredients	Metric	Imperial	American
Dry white wine	75 ml	5 tbsp	5 tbsp
Olive oil	45 ml	3 tbsp	3 tbsp
Garlic cloves, crushed	2	2	2
Bouquet garni	1	1	1
Pinch of sugar			
Pinch of dried tarragon			
Pinch of mustard powder			
Salt and freshly ground black pepper			
Chicken portions	4	4	4
Tarragon Herb Sauce (see page 112)	300 ml	½ pt	1¼ cups

method

1. Mix together all the ingredients except the sauce in a bowl, cover and leave to marinate in the refrigerator overnight.

2. Drain the chicken from the marinade and arrange on a roasting rack with the thickest parts to the outside. Cover and microwave on high for 16-20 minutes until the chicken is cooked through and tender, rearranging twice during cooking.

3. Meanwhile make the herb sauce(see page 112). Transfer the chicken to a serving dish and pour over the sauce. Alternatively you can serve the sauce separately.

Variations

You can substitute different herbs for the tarragon, or you can use turkey pieces for the recipe.

CHICKEN CURRY

ingredients	Metric	Imperial	American
Boned chicken, cut into chunks	350 g	12 oz	¾ lb
Garlic clove, chopped	1	1	1
Plain yoghurt	250 ml	8 fl oz	1 cup
Curry powder	15 ml	1 tbsp	1 tbsp
Pinch of ground cinnamon			
Pinch of ground cloves			
Salt and freshly ground black pepper			
Carrot, sliced	1	1	1
Red pepper, sliced	1	1	1
Chicken stock	250 ml	8 fl oz	1 cup
Cornflour (cornstarch)	30 ml	2 tbsp	2 tbsp

method

1. Place the chicken in a bowl. Mix together the garlic, yoghurt, curry powder, cinnamon and cloves and season with salt and pepper. Pour over the chicken and toss together until thoroughly coated. Cover and chill for 1 hour.

2. Add the carrot and pepper to the chicken then stir in the chicken stock. Cover and microwave on High for 15-20 minutes until the chicken is cooked through and the vegetables are just tender, stirring once or twice during cooking.

3. Mix the cornflour with a little water then stir it into the sauce and microwave on High for 3-4 minutes until the sauce thickens and boils. Serve with rice.

CRISPY CHEESE CHICKEN

ingredients	Metric	Imperial	American
Chicken breasts, boneless	4	4	4
Cheddar cheese	100 g	4 oz	¼ lb
Olive oil	30 ml	2 tbsp	2 tbsp
Garlic clove, crushed	1	1	1
White bread slices, diced	3	3	3
Butter or margarine	15 ml	1 tbsp	1 tbsp
Chopped fresh parsley	15 ml	1 tbsp	1 tbsp
Salt and freshly ground black pepper			

method

1. Place the chicken in a baking dish, cover and microwave on High for 8-12 minutes until the chicken is cooked through, rearranging once during cooking.

2. Cut 4 slices of cheese and finely grate the remainder.

3. Heat the oil in a conventional frying pan and fry the garlic and bread squares until golden brown. Drain, then crush them lightly.

4. Put the butter or margarine in a bowl and microwave on High for 25 seconds until melted. Stir in the fried breadcrumbs and parsley and season with salt and pepper.

5. Lay a slice of cheese on top of each chicken breast and top with the bread mixture, pressing it down lightly. Microwave on High for 1 minute until hot.

CARIBBEAN CHICKEN WINGS

ingredients	Metric	Imperial	American
Chicken wings	450 g	1 lb	1 lb
Canned pineapple chunks	225 g	8 oz	½ lb
Apple, peeled, cored and chopped	1	1	1
Green pepper, diced	1	1	1
Dark brown sugar	50 g	2 oz	¼ cup
Raisins	30 ml	2 tbsp	2 tbsp
Cornflour (cornstarch)	15 ml	1 tbsp	1 tbsp
salt	2.5 ml	½ tsp	½ tsp
Curry powder	2.5 ml	½ tsp	½ tsp
Pinch of ground cinnamon			
Pinch of cayenne pepper			

method

1. Separate the chicken wings into 3 parts at the joints and discard the wing tips.

2. Put the remaining ingredients into a large plastic bag, add the chicken wings and shake to mix. Tie the bag securely and refrigerate overnight, turning the bag over once or twice.

3. Put the chicken and marinade into a casserole dish, cover and microwave on High for 11-13 minutes until the chicken is cooked through and the vegetables are tender, stirring 2 or 3 times during cooking.

CHICKEN AND BROCCOLI WITH CREAM SAUCE

ingredients	Metric	Imperial	American
Broccoli florets	350 g	12 oz	¾ lb
Water	30 ml	2 tbsp	2 tbsp
Carrots, thickly sliced	2	2	2
Chicken breasts, skinned	4	4	4
Butter or margarine	50 g	2 oz	¼ cup
Plain (all-purpose) flour	30 ml	2 tbsp	2 tbsp
Grated lemon rind	5 ml	1 tsp	1 tsp
Pinch of cayenne pepper			
Milk	300 ml	½ pt	1¼ cups
Egg yolks, lightly beaten	2	2	2
Lemon juice	10 ml	2 tsp	2 tsp
Salt and freshly ground black pepper			
Pinch of paprika			

method

1. Place the broccoli and water in a casserole, cover and microwave on High for 4 minutes. Drain.

2. Arrange the carrots on top of the broccoli and place the chicken breasts on top. Cover and microwave on High for 8-10minutes until the chicken is cooked through, rearranging the chicken once during cooking. Drain and cover.

3. Put the butter or margarine into a bowl and microwave on High for 1 minute until melted. Stir in the flour, lemon rind and cayenne then blend in the milk. Microwave on High for 4-5 minutes until the sauce begins to boil and thicken, stirring twice during cooking.

4. Blend a little of the hot sauce into the egg yolks then stir the yolks into the sauce. Microwave on Medium for 1-2 minutes until the mixture thickens, stirring 3 or 4 times during cooking. Stir in the lemon juice and season with salt and pepper.

5. Pour the sauce over the chicken and serve sprinkled with paprika.

CHICKEN IN ORANGE JUICE

ingredients	Metric	Imperial	American
Chicken portions	4	4	4
Orange juice	300 ml	¼ pt	⅔ cup
Garlic clove, finely chopped	1	1	1
Pinch of paprika			
Salt and freshly ground black pepper			
Chopped fresh parsley	15 ml	1 tbsp	1 tbsp
Orange, sliced	1	1	1

method

1. Arrange the chicken pieces in a baking dish with the thickest parts on the outside. Pour over the orange juice and sprinkle with garlic. Season with paprika, salt and pepper.

2. Cover and microwave for 20-25 minutes until the chicken is cooked through, turning and basting the chicken several times during cooking.

3. Leave to stand, covered, for 5 minutes. Sprinkle with parsley and serve garnished with orange slices.

ALMOND TURKEY

ingredients	Metric	Imperial	American
Turkey cutlets	450 g	1 lb	1 lb
Soy sauce	45 ml	3 tbsp	3 tbsp
Garlic clove, crushed	1	1	1
Salt and black pepper			
Butter or margarine	50 g	2 oz	1/4 cup
Flaked almonds	50 g	2 oz	cup
Onion, thinly sliced	1	1	1
Red pepper, chopped	1	1	1
Mushrooms, sliced	100 g	4 oz	1/4 lb
Dry white wine	120 ml	4 fl oz	1/2 cup
Long-grain rice	225 g	8 oz	2/3 cup

method

1. Place the cutlets in a bowl, add the soy sauce and garlic and season with salt and pepper. Stir well, cover and leave to marinate for 30 minutes.

2. Put 15 ml/1 tbsp of butter and the almonds on a plate and microwave on High for 5-6 minutes until golden, stirring occasionally during cooking.

3. Put the rest of the butter, the onion, pepper and mushrooms into a bowl. Cover and microwave on High for 3-4 minutes until tender, stirring once during cooking.

4. Remove the cutlets from the marinade and arrange in a casserole dish. Arrange the vegetables on top, pour in the wine, cover and microwave on Medium for 8-12 minutes until the turkey is cooked through and tender.

5. Meanwhile, cook the rice in boiling salted water on a conventional oven for about 10 minutes until tender. Drain well.

6. Leave the turkey to stand, covered, for 2 minutes before serving with the rice.

TURKEY WITH CIDER AND PEPPERS

ingredients	Metric	Imperial	American
Oil	30 ml	2 tbsp	2 tbsp
Onion, chopped	1	1	1
Boneless turkey, cubed	450 g	1 lb	1 lb
Plain (all-purpose) flour	25 g	1 oz	¼ cup
Dry cider	450 ml	¾ pt	2 cups
Pinch of cayenne pepper			
Salt and freshly ground black pepper			
Canned red peppers, drained and cut into strips	225 g	8 oz	½ lb
Dry sherry	30 ml	2 tbsp	2 tbsp
Double (heavy) cream	30 ml	2 tbsp	2 tbsp
Chopped fresh parsley	15 ml	1 tbsp	1 tbsp

method

1. Place the oil and onion in a casserole dish and microwave on High for 3 minutes.

2. Stir in the turkey and microwave on High for 3 minutes, stirring once during cooking.

3. Stir in the flour and microwave on High for 1 minute.

4. Stir in the cider and season to taste with cayenne, salt and pepper. Cover and microwave on High for 5 minutes, stirring once during cooking. Add the peppers and sherry and microwave on High for 3 minutes until the turkey is cooked through and the sauce is hot.

5. Stir in the cream and serve sprinkled with parsley.

MEAT

BEEF POT ROAST

ingredients	Metric	Imperial	American
Beef topside	1.5 kg	3½ lb	3½ lb
Carrots, chopped	3	3	3
Garlic cloves, crushed	2	2	2
Red wine	120 ml	4 fl oz	½ cup
Water	120 ml	4 fl oz	½ cup
Tomato ketchup (catsup)	45 ml	3 tbsp	3 tbsp
Soy sauce	45 ml	3 tbsp	3 tbsp
Plain (all-purpose) flour	25 g	1 oz	¼ cup
Water	45 ml	3 tbsp	3 tbsp

method

1. Put the beef and carrots into a casserole dish.

2. Mix together the garlic, wine, water, tomato ketchup and soy sauce. Pour over the meat, cover and microwave on Medium for about 1¾ hours until the meat is tender, turning the meat over at least once during cooking.

3. Transfer the meat to a serving plate, cover, and leave to stand.

4. Skim the fat from the casserole dish. Blend the flour and water together to a paste then stir into the stock. Microwave on High for 3-4 minutes until the mixture thickens and bubbles, stirring 3 times during cooking. Serve the gravy with the roast.

BEEF STEW WITH PARSLEY DUMPLINGS

ingredients	Metric	Imperial	American
Plain (all-purpose) flour	45 ml	3 tbsp	3 tbsp
Salt and black pepper			
Stewing steak, cubed	750 g	1½ lb	1½ lb
Onions, sliced	2	2	2
Garlic clove, crushed	1	1	1
Carrots, diced	3	3	3
Canned tomatoes	400 g	14 oz	14 oz
Beef stock	900 ml	1½ pts	3¾ cups
Cornflour (cornstarch)	15 ml	1 tbsp	1 tbsp
For the dumplings:			
Self-raising flour		100 g	4 oz 1 cup
Shredded suet	50 g	2 oz	¼ cup
Chopped fresh parsley	30 ml	2 tbsp	2 tbsp

method

1. Season the flour with salt and pepper then toss the meat in the flour and shake off any excess. Put all the stew ingredients into a large casserole and stir well. Put a small plate on top of the meat to keep the meat and vegetables under the stock. Cover and microwave on High for 8-10 minutes until boiling.

2. Microwave on Low or Simmer for 40-60 minutes.

3. Blend the cornflour to a paste with a little water and stir it into the casserole. Microwave on High for 5 minutes.

4. Meanwhile, mix the flour, suet and parsley and gradually add just enough water to mix to a soft dough. Roll into 2.5 cm/1 in balls.

5. Remove the lid and plate from the casserole. Add the dumplings and microwave on High, uncovered, for 5 minutes.

70

BEEF AND PEPPER STIR-FRY

ingredients	Metric	Imperial	American
New potatoes	450 g	1 lb	1 lb
Green beans, halved	100 g	4 oz	¼ lb
Water	75 ml	5 tbsp	5 tbsp
Oil	45 ml	3 tbsp	3 tbsp
Lean beef, cut into strips	450 g	1 lb	1 lb
Garlic clove, crushed	1	1	1
Red pepper, cut into strips	1	1	1
Cornflour (cornstarch)	10 ml	2 tsp	2 tsp
Beef stock	150 ml	¼ pt	⅔ cup
Worcestershire sauce	15 ml	1 tbsp	1 tbsp
Salt and freshly ground black pepper			

method

1. Place the potatoes, beans and water in a large casserole dish, cover and microwave on High for 6-7 minutes until the potatoes are just tender, stirring once during cooking. Leave to stand, covered, for 5 minutes. Drain.

2. Thickly slice the potatoes and return them to the dish with the oil. Stir gently.

3. Heat the oil in a conventional frying pan and brown the beef lightly. Add the garlic and pepper and fry until just browned.

4. Transfer the beef and pepper to the casserole dish. Mix together the cornflour, stock and Worcestershire sauce and season to taste with salt and pepper. Cover and microwave on High for 5-7 minutes until the meat is cooked and the sauce has thickened, stirring twice during cooking. Serve with rice or noodles.

BEEF WITH BROCCOLI

ingredients	Metric	Imperial	American
Lean beef, cut into strips	450 g	1 lb	1 lb
Plain (all-purpose) flour	15 ml	1 tbsp	1 tbsp
Spring onions (scallions), sliced	6	6	6
Grated fresh ginger root	5 ml	1 tsp	1 tsp
Garlic clove, crushed	1	1	1
Beef stock	120 ml	4 fl oz	½ cup
Soy sauce	75 ml	5 tbsp	5 tbsp
Honey	45 ml	3 tbsp	3 tbsp
Dry sherry	15 ml	1 tbsp	1 tbsp
Carrots, sliced	225 g	8 oz	½ lb
Broccoli florets	225 g	8 oz	½ lb

method

1. Toss the beef in the flour then mix with the spring onions, ginger and garlic. Blend together the stock, soy sauce, honey and sherry, pour over the meat mixture, cover and refrigerate for at least 3 hours.

2. Place the meat mixture in a casserole dish and stir in the carrots. Cover and microwave on High for 5 minutes, then microwave on Medium for 30 minutes.

3. Stir in the broccoli, cover and microwave on Medium for a further 5-8 minutes until the meat is tender and the vegetables are just tender but still crisp. Leave to stand for 5 minutes before serving.

CHILLI CON CARNE

ingredients	Metric	Imperial	American
Onions, chopped	2	2	2
Garlic clove, crushed	1	1	1
Minced (ground) beef	675 g	1½ lb	1½ lb
Canned tomatoes	800 g	1¾ lb	1¾ lb
Canned red kidney beans, drained	800 g	1¾ lb	1¾ lb
Beef stock	120 ml	4 fl oz	½ cup
Chilli powder	30 ml	2 tbsp	2 tbsp
Worcestershire sauce	15 ml	1 tbsp	1 tbsp
Sugar	5 ml	1 tsp	1 tsp
Salt	5 ml	1 tsp	1 tsp
Ground cumin	5 ml	1 tsp	1 tsp
Pinch of cayenne pepper			
Salt and freshly ground black pepper			

method

1. Put the onion and garlic in a casserole dish, cover and microwave on High for 2-3 minutes until tender.

2. Stir in the beef, cover and microwave on High for 5-6 minutes until the beef is browned, stirring twice during cooking. Drain off any excess fat.

3. Stir in the remaining ingredients, seasoning the mixture to taste. Microwave on High for 10 minutes then stir well. Microwave on Medium for 20-25 minutes until the meat is cooked and the flavours have blended, stirring at least twice during cooking.

STUFFED PEPPERS

ingredients	Metric	Imperial	American
Red or green peppers	4	4	4
Minced (ground) beef	450 g	1 lb	1 lb
Onion, sliced	1	1	1
Red wine or stock	150 ml	¼ pt	⅔ cup
Tomato purée (paste)	30 ml	2 tbsp	2 tbsp
Cornflour (cornstarch)	15 ml	1 tbsp	1 tbsp
Dried mixed herbs	5 ml	1 tsp	1 tsp
Gruyère cheese, grated	100 g	4 oz	½ cup

method

1. Slice a lid off the top of each pepper and put it aside. Scoop out and discard the seeds and pith.

2. Mix together the beef, onion, wine or stock, tomato purée, cornflour and herbs in a bowl, cover and microwave on Medium for 18-20 minutes. Leave to cool slightly.

3. Fill the peppers with the mixture and replace the lids. Arrange on a dish, cover and microwave on High for 10-12 minutes until soft.

4. Sprinkle with the cheese and microwave on High for 3-5 minutes until the cheese has melted.

BEEFBURGERS

ingredients	Metric	Imperial	American
Minced (ground) beef	450 g	1 lb	1 lb
Finely chopped onion	15 ml	1 tbsp	1 tbsp
Worcestershire sauce	5 ml	1 tsp	1 tsp
Salt and freshly ground black pepper			
Soft round rolls	4	4	4
To garnish:			
Lettuce			
Tomato slices			
Gherkin slices			

method

1. Mix together the beef, onion and Worcestershire sauce and season with salt and pepper.

2. Shape the mixture into 4 burgers. Stand the burgers on a microwave rack and microwave on High for 5-7 minutes until the meat is firm and browned, turning once during cooking.

3. Cover and leave to stand for 3 minutes.

4. Slit open the rolls and lightly toast the insides. Fill with the burgers and garnish with lettuce, tomato and gherkin.

MEATLOAF WITH VEGETABLES

ingredients	Metric	Imperial	American
Minced (ground) beef	450 g	1 lb	1 lb
Onion, finely chopped	1	1	1
Garlic clove, crushed	1	1	1
Dried breadcrumbs	50 g	2 oz	¼ cup
Worcestershire sauce	5 ml	1 tsp	1 tsp
Tomato purée (paste)	15 ml	1 tbsp	1 tbsp
Salt and freshly ground black pepper			
Potatoes, diced	225 g	8 oz	½ lb
Carrots, diced	3	3	3
Celery stalks, sliced	2	2	2
Button onions	6	6	6
Beef stock	150 ml	¼ pt	⅓ cup
Red wine	75 ml	5 tbsp	5 tbsp

method

1. Mix together the beef, onion, garlic, breadcrumbs, Worcestershire sauce and tomato purée and season with salt and pepper. Press the mixture into a loaf tin then turn it out into a large casserole dish.

2. Arrange the vegetables around the meatloaf. Mix together the stock and wine and pour over the meat and vegetables. Cover and microwave on High for 30-35 minutes until the meatloaf is firm and cooked through and the vegetables are tender, stirring twice during cooking. Leave to stand, covered, for 10 minutes before serving.

HUNGARIAN GOULASH

ingredients	Metric	Imperial	American
Minced (ground) beef	450 g	1 lb	1 lb
Green pepper, chopped	1	1	1
Onion, chopped	1	1	1
Garlic clove, chopped	1	1	1
Canned chopped tomatoes	400 g	14 oz	14 oz
Tomato purée (paste)	30 ml	2 tbsp	2 tbsp
Macaroni	100 g	4 oz	¼ lb
Salt and freshly ground black pepper			

method

1. Mix together the beef, pepper, onion and garlic and microwave on High for 6-8 minutes until the meat is browned, stirring once or twice during cooking. Drain off any excess fat.

2. Stir in the remaining ingredients and season with salt and pepper. Cover and microwave on High for 18-20 minutes until the macaroni is tender and the flavours are well blended, stirring regularly during cooking.

3. Leave to stand, covered, for 5 minutes before serving.

PORK WITH WHITE WINE SAUCE

ingredients	Metric	Imperial	American
Butter or margarine	15 ml	1 tbsp	1 tbsp
Onions, sliced	2	2	2
Garlic clove, crushed	1	1	1
Plain (all-purpose) flour	30 ml	2 tbsp	2 tbsp
Salt and freshly ground black pepper			
Pork chops	4	4	4
Dry white wine	120 ml	4 fl oz	½ cup
Soy sauce	30 ml	2 tbsp	2 tbsp
Chopped fresh parsley	30 ml	2 tbsp	2 tbsp

method

1. Put the butter or margarine, onions and garlic into a casserole dish, cover and microwave on High for 3-4 minutes until the onions are soft.

2. Season the flour generously with salt and pepper and coat the chops in the seasoned flour. Stir any excess flour into the onion mixture then place the chops on top.

3. Mix together the wine and soy sauce, pour over the chops, cover and microwave on High for 3 minutes. Microwave on Medium for 15-20 minutes until the chops are cooked through, turning the chops once and spoon the sauce over the chops once or twice during cooking.

4. Leave to stand, covered, for 3 minutes. Serve sprinkled with parsley.

MARINATED CHINESE-STYLE PORK CHOPS

ingredients	Metric	Imperial	American
Pork chops	4	4	4
Soft brown sugar	45 ml	3 tbsp	3 tbsp
Soy sauce	30 ml	2 tbsp	2 tbsp
Dry white wine	30 ml	2 tbsp	2 tbsp
Pinch of mustard powder			
Pinch of five-spice powder			
Oil	15 ml	1 tbsp	1 tbsp
Quick-cook long-grain rice	100 g	4 oz	1 cup
Chicken stock	250 ml	8 fl oz	1 cup
Canned pineapple chunks, drained	225 g	8 oz	½ lb
Spring onions (scallions), sliced	6	6	6
Red pepper, chopped	1	1	1
Soy sauce	15 ml	1 tbsp	1 tbsp

method

1. Place the chops in a bowl. Mix together the sugar, soy sauce, wine, mustard and five-spice powder and pour over the chops. Cover and leave to marinate for at least 6 hours.

2. Drain the chops and discard the marinade.

3. Heat the oil in a conventional frying pan and fry the chops until lightly browned on both sides.

4. Mix together the remaining ingredients and place in a casserole dish. Arrange the chops on top, cover and microwave on Medium for 12-15 minutes until the meat is cooked through and the rice is tender, stirring twice during cooking.

PORK WITH PEPPERS

ingredients	Metric	Imperial	American
Onion, thickly sliced	1	1	1
Dry white wine	75 ml	5 tbsp	5 tbsp
Oil	15 ml	1 tbsp	1 tbsp
Garlic clove, crushed	1	1	1
Dried thyme	2.5 ml	½ tsp	½ tsp
Chopped fresh parsley	15 ml	1 tbsp	1 tbsp
Lean pork, cut into strips	450 g	1 lb	1 lb
Green pepper, cut into chunks	1	1	1
Red pepper, cut into chunks	1	1	1
Yellow pepper, cut into chunks	1	1	1
Salt and freshly ground black pepper			
Cornflour (cornstarch)	5 ml	1 tsp	1 tsp

method

1. Place the onion, wine, oil, garlic, thyme and parsley in a casserole, cover and microwave on High for 5 minutes until the onion is just soft.

2. Add the pork and peppers, cover and microwave on Medium for 6-8 minutes until the pork is cooked through, stirring twice during cooking. Season to taste with salt and pepper.

3. Blend the cornflour to a paste with a little water, stir it in to the mixture and microwave on High for 12 minutes until the sauce is thick and clear, stirring several times during cooking.

4. Toss the ingredients well before serving.

PORK WITH PLUMS

ingredients	Metric	Imperial	American
Boned and rolled loin of pork	1.5 kg	3 lb	3 lb
Butter or margarine	30 ml	2 tbsp	2 tbsp
Onion, sliced	1	1	1
Tomato pureé (paste)	30 ml	2 tbsp	2 tbsp
Soft brown sugar	50 g	2 oz	¼ cup
Plums, stoned	800 g	1¾ lb	1¾ lb
Cornflour (cornstarch)	15 ml	1 tbsp	1 tbsp
Dry red wine	150 ml	¼ pt	⅔ cup

method

1. Place the joint in a shallow dish and microwave on High for 15 minutes. Shield the ends with a little foil and microwave on High for 15 minutes. Wrap tightly in foil and leave to stand for 20 minutes.

2. Place the butter or margarine, onion, tomato pureé and sugar in a bowl, cover and microwave on High for 4 minutes, stirring once during cooking. stir in the plums.

3. Blend the cornflour to a paste with the wine, stir into the dish, cover and cook on High for 9 minutes, stirring once during cooking.

4. Slice the pork and arrange on a serving dish. Spoon over a little plum sauce and serve the rest separately.

PORK WITH WINTER VEGETABLES

ingredients	Metric	Imperial	American
Onion, sliced	1	1	1
Carrots, cut into strips	2	2	2
Turnip, cut into strips	1	1	1
Small suede (rutabaga), cut into strips	1	1	1
Chicken stock	120 ml	4 fl oz	½ cup
Pork chops	4	4	4
Rosemary sprig	1	1	1
Chopped fresh parsley	15 ml	1 tbsp	1 tbsp
Soft brown sugar	10 ml	2 tsp	2 tsp
Salt and pepper			
Cornflour (cornstarch) (optional)	5 ml	1 tsp	1 tsp

method

1. Place the onion, carrots, turnip and suede in a casserole dish and spoon over 45 ml/3 tbsp of stock. Cover and microwave on High for 6-8 minutes until the vegetables are almost tender, stirring once during cooking.

2. Arrange the pork chops on top of the vegetables with the thickest portions to the outside and place the rosemary sprig on top.

3. Mix the remaining stock with the parsley and sugar and season with salt and pepper. Pour over the chops, cover and microwave on Medium for 12-15 minutes until the pork is cooked through. Leave to stand, covered, for 5 minutes.

4. If you prefer a thicker sauce, blend the cornflour to a paste with a little cold water. Lift the meat and vegetables from the sauce and arrange them on a warm serving plate. Stir the cornflour into the

sauce, cover and microwave on High for 1-2 minutes until the sauce is thick and clear, stirring once or twice during cooking.

PORK WITH CIDER

ingredients	Metric	Imperial	American
Butter or margarine	30 ml	2 tbsp	2 tbsp
Onions, chopped	2	2	2
Pork fillet, cubed	450 g	1 lb	1 lb
Mushrooms, sliced	100g	4 oz	¼ lb
Dry cider	300 ml	½ pt	1¼ cups
Salt and freshly ground black pepper			
Cornflour (cornstarch)	30 ml	2 tbsp	2 tbsp
Water	15 ml	1 tbsp	1 tbsp
Double (heavy) cream	15 ml	1 tbsp	1tbsp

method

1. Place the butter or margarine and onion in a dish and microwave on High for 3 minutes. Add the pork and microwave on High for 5 minutes, stirring several times.

2. Add the mushrooms, cider, salt and pepper, cover and microwave on High for 8-10 minutes until the pork is tender, stirring once or twice during cooking.

3. Blend the cornflour with the water, stir it into the casserole and microwave on High for 2 minutes until thickened. Stir in the cream before serving.

SWEET AND SOUR PORK

ingredients	Metric	Imperial	American
Lean pork, cubed	450 g	1 lb	1 lb
Onion, quartered	1	1	1
Garlic clove, crushed	1	1	1
Carrot, sliced	2	2	2
Green pepper, diced	1	1	1
Canned bamboo shoots, drained	200 g	7 oz	7 oz
For the sauce:			
Sugar	50 g	2 oz	1/4 cup
Cornflour (cornstarch)	15 ml	1 tbsp	1 tbsp
Canned pineapple chunks	225 g	8 oz	1/2 lb
Tomato ketchup (catsup)	45 ml	3 tbsp	3 tbsp
White wine	30 ml	2 tbsp	2 tbsp
White wine vinegar	45 ml	2 tbsp	2 tbsp
Grated ginger root	2.5 ml	1/2 tsp	1/2 tsp
Salt and freshly ground black pepper			

method

1. Place the pork in a casserole dish, cover and microwave on High for 5-6 minutes until cooked through, stirring once during cooking. Transfer the pork to a bowl and drain off the fat.

2. Place the onion, garlic, carrot, pepper and bamboo shoots in the casserole, cover and microwave on High for 5-6 minutes until just tender, stirring once during cooking. Stir the pork back into the casserole.

3. Mix the sauce ingredients together in a jug and microwave on High for 5-6 minutes until thick and clear, stirring once or twice during cooking. Pour

over the vegetables and pork and stir well. Cover
and microwave on High for 2-3 minutes until
heated through, stirring once during cooking.
Serve with rice.

SPICED FRUIT LAMB

ingredients	Metric	Imperial	American
Butter or margarine	25 g	1 oz	2 tbsp
Onion, sliced	1	1	1
Garlic clove, chopped	1	1	1
Whole almonds	25 g	1 oz	1/4 cup
Button mushrooms	100 g	4 oz	1/4 lb
Plain (all-purpose) flour	30 ml	2 tbsp	2 tbsp
Ground allspice	2.5 ml	1/2 tsp	1/2 tsp
Ground cumin	10 ml	2 tsp	2 tsp
Salt and freshly ground black pepper			
Tomato purée (paste)	30 ml	2 tbsp	2 tbsp
Beef stock	300 ml	1/2 pt	1 1/4 cups
Lean lamb, cubed	450 g	1 lb	1 lb
Dried apricots	50 g	2 oz	1/3 cup

method

1. Place the butter or margarine, onion, garlic,
    almonds and mushrooms in a casserole dish and
    microwave on High for 3 minutes.

2. Stir in the flour, all-spice and cumin and season
    with salt and pepper.

3. Stir in the tomato purée and stock and add the
    lamb and apricots. Stir well, cover and microwave
    on Low for 45-50 minutes until the meat is tender.
    Leave to stand, covered, for 5 minutes before
    serving with rice.

Eggs and Cheese

SCRAMBLED EGGS

Serves 1

ingredients	Metric	Imperial	American
Butter or margarine	*15 ml*	*1 tbsp*	*1 tbsp*
Eggs	*2*	*2*	*2*
Milk	*30 ml*	*2 tbsp*	*2 tbsp*
Salt and freshly ground black pepper			
Chopped fresh chives	*15 ml*	*1 tbsp*	*1 tbsp*

method

1. Place the butter or margarine in a jug and microwave on High for 30 seconds until melted.

2. Stir in the eggs and milk and season with salt and pepper. Microwave on High for 1-1½ minutes until creamy, stirring once during cooking.

3. Stir in the chives and leave to stand for 2 minutes until firm.

POACHED EGGS

Serves 1

ingredients	Metric	Imperial	American
Water	150 ml	¼ pt	⅔ cup
Few drops of vinegar			
Pinch of salt			
Egg	1	1	1

method

1. Place the water, vinegar and salt in a ramekin dish and microwave on High for 1½ minutes.

2. Add the egg and use a cocktail stick (toothpick) to pierce the yolk twice and the white several times. Cover with plastic wrap and microwave on Medium for 30-45 seconds.

3. Leave to stand, covered, for 1 minute before serving.

Quiche Lorraine

ingredients	Metric	Imperial	American
Butter or margarine	25 g	1 oz	2 tbsp
Onion, chopped	1	1	1
Red pepper, sliced	½	½	½
Cooked 23 cm/9 in shortcrust pastry case (see page 152)			
Bacon rashers (slices), rinded and chopped	4	4	4
Cheddar cheese, grated	100 g	4 oz	1 cup
Eggs, beaten	2	2	2
Milk	300 ml	½ pt	1¼ cups
Mixed herbs	5 ml	1 tsp	1 tsp

method

1. Place the butter or margarine in a bowl and microwave on High for 45 seconds until melted. Stir in the onion and pepper and microwave on High for 2 minutes. Spoon into the pastry case.

2. Sprinkle the bacon into the pastry case and sprinkle over the cheese.

3. Beat together the eggs, most of the milk and the herbs. Pour into the flan, adding the remaining milk to fill the flan, if necessary.

4. Cover and microwave on Low for 10-12 minutes until the centre is firm. Serve hot or cold.

SPAGHETTI CARBONARA

ingredients	Metric	Imperial	American
Bacon rashers (slices), rinded	4	4	4
Spaghetti	350 g	12 oz	¾ lb
Salt			
Olive oil	15 ml	1 tbsp	1 tbsp
Butter or margarine	50 g	2 oz	¼ cup
Parmesan cheese, grated	50 g	2 oz	½ cup
Eggs, beaten	2	2	2
Single (light) cream	120 ml	4 fl oz	½ cup
Freshly ground black pepper			

method

1. Place the bacon on a plate lined with kitchen paper. Cover and microwave on High for 3-5 minutes until crisp. Leave to cool slightly then crumble or chop.

2. Cook the spaghetti in boiling salted water with the olive oil on a conventional oven for about 8 minutes until tender. Drain well then return to the hot saucepan, cover and keep warm.

3. Put the butter or margarine in a casserole dish and microwave on Medium for 15-30 seconds until softened. Stir in the bacon, cheese, eggs and cream and season with pepper. Stir in the spaghetti, tossing well to coat with the sauce. Microwave on Medium for 3-4 minutes until heated through, stirring twice during cooking.

MACARONI CHEESE

ingredients	Metric	Imperial	American
Macaroni	225 g	8 oz	2 cups
Salt			
Oil	15 ml	1 tbsp	1 tbsp
Boiling water			
Butter or margarine	50 g	2 oz	1/4 cup
Plain (all-purpose) flour	50 g	2 oz	1/2 cup
Milk	600 ml	1 pt	2 1/2 cups
Freshly ground black pepper			
Cheddar cheese, grated	225 g	8 oz	2 cups
Tomatoes, skinned and sliced	2	2	2

method

1. Place the macaroni, 5 ml/1 tsp of salt and the oil in a large bowl and cover with boiling water. Microwave on High for 12 minutes. Leave to stand for 3 minutes then drain.

2. Place the butter or margarine in a large jug and microwave on High for 1 minute until melted. Stir in the flour until smooth. Whisk in the milk and microwave on High for 3-4 minutes until boiled and thickened, stirring twice during cooking.

3. Stir half the cheese into the sauce and season with salt and pepper.

4. Place the macaroni in a casserole dish and stir in the cheese sauce. Arrange the tomatoes on top and sprinkle with the remaining cheese. Microwave on High for 3-4 minutes. Finish under a conventional grill (broiler), if liked.

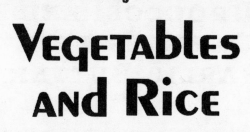

VEGETABLES AND RICE

LEMON ASPARAGUS

ingredients	Metric	Imperial	American
Asparagus, trimmed	450 g	1 lb	1 lb
Lemon, thinly sliced	1	1	1
Button mushrooms, halved	100 g	4 oz	¼ lb
Chicken stock or water	45 ml	3 tbsp	3 tbsp
Dry white wine or water	45 ml	3 tbsp	3 tbsp

method

1. Lay a piece of kitchen paper on a plate and arrange half the lemon slices on the paper. Arrange the asparagus spears in a single layer on top and finish with the remaining lemon. Arrange the mushrooms around the edge of the plate. Cover with a second piece of kitchen paper.

2. Mix together the stock and wine and pour over the kitchen paper. Microwave on High for 7-10 minutes until the asparagus is just tender, rearranging once during cooking. Leave to stand for 3 minutes before serving.

BROCCOLI AND CARROTS WITH GARLIC BUTTER

ingredients	Metric	Imperial	American
Broccoli florets	225 g	8 oz	½ lb
Carrots, thinly sliced	225 g	8 oz	½ lb
Chopped fresh thyme	10 ml	2 tsp	2 tsp
Butter or margarine	50 g	2 oz	¼ cup
Small garlic clove, crushed			
Chopped fresh parsley	5 ml	1 tsp	1 tsp
Few drops of lemon juice			

method

1. Lay a piece of kitchen paper on a plate and arrange the broccoli and carrots on top. Sprinkle with thyme. Lay another piece of kitchen paper on top then pour enough water on to the paper towel to moisten it thoroughly.

2. Microwave on High for 3-5 minutes until the vegetables are just tender. Leave to stand for 3 minutes.

3. Meanwhile, mix the butter or margarine with garlic, parsley and lemon juice to taste. Arrange the vegetables on a serving dish and top with pats of the garlic butter.

BRUSSELS SPROUTS WITH LEMON BUTTER

ingredients	Metric	Imperial	American
Brussels sprouts	450 g	1 lb	1 lb
Hot water	120 ml	4 fl oz	½ cup
Butter or margarine	100 g	4 oz	½ cup
Grated lemon rind	15 ml	1 tbsp	1 tbsp
Lemon juice	15 ml	1 tbsp	1 tbsp
Salt and freshly ground black pepper			

method

1. Place the sprouts and water in a casserole dish, cover and microwave on High for 6-8 minutes until just tender, stirring once during cooking.

2. Place the butter or margarine in a bowl and microwave on High for 45 seconds until melted. Stir in the lemon rind and juice and season to taste with salt and pepper.

3. Drain the sprouts well and place in a warmed serving dish. Pour over the lemon butter and toss until well coated.

CABBAGE WITH BACON

ingredients	Metric	Imperial	American
Head of cabbage, trimmed and shredded	1	1	1
Water	30 ml	2 tbsp	2 tbsp
Butter or margarine	50 g	2 oz	1/4 cup
Onions, sliced	2	2	2
Bacon rashers (slices), rinded	4	4	4
Salt and freshly ground black pepper			
Pinch of grated nutmeg			

method

1. Place the cabbage in a casserole dish, sprinkle with water, cover and microwave on High for 8-10 minutes until the cabbage is just tender but still crisp, stirring once or twice during cooking.

2. Place the butter or margarine in a large bowl and microwave on High for 45 seconds until melted. Stir in the onions and microwave on High for 2-3 minutes until soft, stirring once during cooking.

3. Arrange the bacon on a sheet of kitchen paper and microwave on High for about 4 minutes until crisp.

4. Chop the bacon and mix it with the onions. Stir the mixture into the cabbage, season with salt and pepper and microwave on High for 2 minutes until heated through and blended. Serve sprinkled with nutmeg.

MINTED CARROTS AND SPROUTS

ingredients	Metric	Imperial	American
Brussels sprouts	450 g	1 lb	1 lb
Baby carrots	450 g	1 lb	1 lb
Hot water	45 ml	3 tbsp	3 tbsp
Butter or margarine	50 g	2 oz	¼ cup
Dry white wine	30 ml	2 tbsp	2 tbsp
Chopped fresh mint	10 ml	2 tsp	2 tsp

method

1. Place the sprouts and carrots in a casserole dish and add the water. Cover and microwave on High for 6-8 minutes until the vegetables are tender, stirring once or twice during cooking. Drain.

2. Place the butter or margarine, wine and half the mint in a bowl and microwave on High for 1 minute until bubbling. Pour over the vegetables and toss together well until coated with flavoured butter. Reheat on High for 12 minutes then serve sprinkled with the remaining mint.

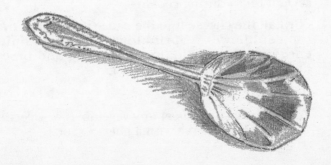

CAULIFLOWER AU GRATIN

ingredients	Metric	Imperial	American
Cauliflower, broken into florets	1	1	1
Water	15 ml	1 tbsp	1 tbsp
Butter or margarine	25 g	1 oz	2 tbsp
Plain (all-purpose) flour	30 ml	2 tbsp	2 tbsp
Milk	300 ml	½ pt	1¼ cups
Salt and freshly ground black pepper			
Cheddar cheese, grated	100 g	4 oz	1 cup
Pinch of grated nutmeg			

method

1. Put the cauliflower in a casserole dish, sprinkle with water, cover and microwave on High for 6-7 minutes until just tender.

2. Put the butter or margarine into a bowl and microwave on High for 45 seconds until melted. Stir in the flour and microwave on High for 20 seconds. Blend in the milk and season with salt and pepper. Microwave on High for 2-3 minutes until the mixture thickens and bubbles, stirring several times during cooking.

3. Stir half the cheese into the sauce and pour it over the cauliflower. Sprinkle with the remaining cheese and a sprinkling of nutmeg and brown under a conventional grill (broiler).

Variations

You can prepare almost any vegetables or selection of vegetables to serve with a cheese sauce.

STUFFED MARROW

ingredients	Metric	Imperial	American
Olive oil	15 ml	1 tbsp	1 tbsp
Onion, chopped	1	1	1
Garlic clove, crushed	1	1	1
Mushrooms, chopped	100 g	4 oz	¼ lb
Dried mixed herbs	5 ml	1 tsp	1 tsp
Cooked long-grain rice	100 g	4 oz	½ cup
Salt and freshly ground black pepper			
Marrow	1	1	1
Chicken or vegetable stock	60 ml	4 tbsp	4 tbsp
Tomato Sauce (see page 119)			

method

1. Place the oil, onion and garlic in a bowl and microwave on High for 2-3 minutes until the onion is soft, stirring once or twice during cooking.

2. Add the mushrooms and herbs and microwave on High for 1 minute, stirring once during cooking.

3. Stir in the rice and season to taste with salt and pepper.

4. Meanwhile, peel and trim the marrow and cut it into 5 cm/2 in slices. Hollow out the centres and arrange in a large baking dish.

5. Fill the marrow slices with the stuffing and spoon over the stock. Cover and microwave on High for 6-8 minutes until tender, rearranging and basting once during cooking.

6. Leave to stand for 3 minutes then serve with tomato sauce.

CREAMY MUSHROOMS

ingredients	Metric	Imperial	American
Button mushrooms	225 g	8 oz	½ lb
Water	15 ml	1 tbsp	1 tbsp
Butter or margarine	25 g	1 oz	2 tbsp
Small onion, chopped	1	1	1
Garlic clove, chopped	1	1	1
Double (heavy) cream	150 ml	¼ pt	⅔ cup
Brandy	30 ml	2 tbsp	2 tbsp
Chopped fresh parsley	15 ml	1 tbsp	1 tbsp

method

1. Place the mushrooms in a casserole dish and sprinkle with the water. Microwave on High for 5-8 minutes until tender.

2. Place the butter or margarine, onion and garlic in a bowl and microwave on High for 2 minutes until the onion is soft, stirring once during cooking.

3. Stir in the cream and brandy and microwave on High for 2 minutes until warm. Pour over the mushrooms and serve sprinkled with parsley.

SUGAR-GLAZED ONIONS

ingredients	Metric	Imperial	American
Soft brown sugar	45 ml	2 tbsp	2 tbsp
Cornflour (cornstarch)	15 ml	1 tbsp	1 tbsp
Pinch of mustard powder			
Salt and freshly ground black pepper			
White wine vinegar	45 ml	3 tbsp	3 tbsp
Hot water	75 ml	5 tbsp	5 tbsp
Small white onions, quartered	10	10	10

method

1. Mix together the sugar, cornflour, mustard, salt and pepper. Gradually blend in the wine vinegar and water until smooth. Microwave on High for 1-2 minutes until thickened, stirring once during cooking.

2. Place the onions in a casserole dish, pour over the sauce and stir well. Microwave on High for 6-8 minutes until just tender, stirring several times during cooking. Leave to stand for 4 minutes before serving.

POTATOES LYONNAISE

ingredients

ingredients	Metric	Imperial	American
Potatoes, sliced	450 g	1 lb	1 lb
Plain (all-purpose) flour	30 ml	2 tbsp	2 tbsp
Butter or margarine, melted	25 g	1 oz	2 tbsp
Milk	150 ml	¼ pt	⅔ cup
Salt and freshly ground black pepper			
Chopped fresh chives	15 ml	1 tbsp	1 tbsp

method

1. Toss the potatoes in the flour then arrange them in a casserole dish.

2. Whisk the butter or margarine and the remaining flour into the milk and season to taste with salt and pepper. Pour the mixture over the potatoes.

3. Cover and cook on Medium for 10-15 minutes. Leave to stand for 5 minutes before serving sprinkled with the chives.

DUCHESSE POTATOES

ingredients	Metric	Imperial	American
Potatoes, peeled and halved	450 g	1 lb	1 lb
Hot water	75 ml	5 tbsp	5 tbsp
Salt and freshly ground black pepper			
Butter or margarine, softened	50 g	2 oz	¼ cup
Double (heavy) cream	60 ml	4 tbsp	4 tbsp
Chopped fresh chives	5 ml	1 tsp	1 tsp
Milk	250 ml	8 fl oz	1 cup
Paprika			

method

1. Place the potatoes, water and salt in a bowl, cover and microwave on High for 8-10 minutes until tender, stirring once or twice during cooking.

2. Drain and mash the potatoes. Mix in the butter or margarine, cream and chives and season to taste with salt and pepper. Gradually add just enough milk to give a smooth consistency.

3. Pipe rosettes of the potato on to a baking sheet lined with greaseproof paper. Sprinkle with paprika. Cover with greaseproof paper and microwave on Medium for 1-2 minutes until reheated.

BAKED POTATOES WITH BACON AND ONIONS

ingredients	Metric	Imperial	American
Baking potatoes	4	4	4
Bacon rashers (slices), rinded	4	4	4
Butter or margarine	50 g	2 oz	¼ cup
Spring onions (scallions), sliced	6	6	6
Single (light) cream	75 ml	5 tbsp	5 tbsp
Paprika			
Salt and freshly ground black pepper			

method

1. Prick the potatoes with a fork, place on a sheet of kitchen paper and microwave on High for 10-12 minutes until soft, rearranging once during cooking. Leave to stand for 5 minutes.

2. Arrange the bacon on a sheet of kitchen paper and microwave on High for 5-6 minutes until crisp. Chop the bacon.

3. Place the butter or margarine in a bowl and microwave on High for 45 seconds until melted. Stir in the spring onions and microwave on High for 1-2 minutes until the onions are softened.

4. Cut the potatoes in half lengthways, then scoop out and mash the flesh. Mix with the bacon and onions then blend in the cream and season to taste with paprika, salt and pepper.

5. Pile the mixture back into the potato shells and microwave on High for 3-5 minutes until reheated, rearranging once during cooking.

POTATO SALAD

ingredients	Metric	Imperial	American
New potatoes, diced	225 g	8 oz	½ lb
Water	15 ml	1 tbsp	1 tbsp
Spring onions (scallions), chopped	3	3	3
Mayonnaise	150 ml	¼ pt	⅔ cup
Milk	15 ml	1 tbsp	1 tbsp
Salt and freshly ground black pepper			

method

1. Place the potatoes and water in a bowl, cover and microwave on High for 4-6 minutes until just tender, stirring twice during cooking.

2. Leave to stand for 2 minutes then leave to cool.

3. Stir in the spring onions.

4. Mix together the mayonnaise and milk and stir into the potatoes. Season to taste with salt and pepper.

RATATOUILLE

ingredients	Metric	Imperial	American
Olive oil	30 ml	2 tbsp	2 tbsp
Onions, sliced	2	2	2
Garlic cloves, chopped	2	2	2
Aubergines (eggplants), thinly sliced	2	2	2
Green pepper, thinly sliced	1	1	1
Red pepper, thinly sliced	1	1	1
Chilli pepper (optional)	1	1	1
Courgettes (zucchini), thinly sliced	3	3	3
Canned tomatoes, drained and coarsely chopped	750 g	1½ lb	1½ lb
Paprika	5 ml	1 tsp	1 tsp
Dried basil	5 ml	1 tsp	1 tsp
Tomato purée (paste)	15 ml	1 tbsp	1 tbsp
Brown sugar	5 ml	1 tsp	1 tsp
Salt and freshly ground black pepper			

method

1. Put the oil, onions and garlic in a bowl and microwave on High for 5 minutes.

2. Stir in the aubergines, peppers, chilli pepper, if using, courgettes, tomatoes, paprika, basil, tomato purée and sugar. Cover and microwave on High for 18-20 minutes, stirring twice during cooking.

3. Remove the lid and season with salt and pepper. Microwave on Medium for 5-6 minutes.

GARLIC-BUTTERED SWEETCORN

ingredients	Metric	Imperial	American
Sweetcorn cobs	4	4	4
Water	120 ml	4 fl oz	½ cup
Butter or margarine	100 g	4 oz	½ cup
Garlic cloves, crushed	2	2	2
Salt and freshly ground black pepper			
Pinch of grated nutmeg			

method

1. Place the corn in a dish with the water and place a knob of butter on each corn cob. Cover and microwave on High for 8-10 minutes until tender, turning over half way through cooking.

2. Place the remaining butter in a bowl with the garlic and microwave on High for 2 minutes. Season with salt and pepper.

3. Transfer the corn to a serving plate, brush over a little of the garlic butter and sprinkle with nutmeg. Serve the remaining garlic butter separately.

VEGETABLE SELECTION WITH BUTTER SAUCE

ingredients	Metric	Imperial	American
Fresh asparagus, trimmed	*450 g*	*1 lb*	*1 lb*
Button mushrooms	*100 g*	*4 oz*	*4 oz*
Courgettes (zucchini), sliced	*2*	*2*	*2*
Carrots, sliced	*2*	*2*	*2*
Water	*45 ml*	*3 tbsp*	*3 tbsp*
Few drops of lemon juice			
Butter or margarine	*50 g*	*2 oz*	*¼ cup*
Salt and freshly ground black pepper			

method

1. Arrange the asparagus in the centre of a large plate. Arrange the mushrooms in a circle around them, then the courgettes and carrots. The vegetables which need the most cooking time should be nearest to the edge. Sprinkle with water and lemon juice, cover and microwave on High for 7-9 minutes until the vegetables are tender. Leave to stand while preparing the butter sauce.

2. Put the butter or margarine in a small bowl and microwave on High for 2-3 minutes until golden brown. Spoon over the vegetables before serving.

RICE WITH PARSLEY

ingredients	Metric	Imperial	American
Butter or margarine	15 ml	1 tbsp	1 tbsp
Onion, chopped	1	1	1
Dried basil	5 ml	1 tsp	1 tsp
Hot water	750 ml	1¼ pts	3 cups
Long-grain rice	350 g	12 oz	1½ cups
Chopped fresh parsley	75 ml	5 tbsp	5 tbsp
Salt and freshly ground black pepper			

method

1. Place the butter or margarine, onion and basil in a casserole dish, cover and microwave on High for 2-3 minutes until the onion is soft, stirring once during cooking.

2. Stir in the remaining ingredients, cover and microwave on High for 5 minutes, then microwave on Medium for 14-18 minutes until the rice is tender and the liquid has been absorbed, stirring once or twice during cooking.

3. Leave to stand, covered, for 5-6 minutes then fluff with a fork before serving.

HERB-FLAVOURED RICE

ingredients	Metric	Imperial	American
Butter or margarine	25 g	1 oz	2 tbsp
Onion, finely chopped	1	1	1
Garlic clove, crushed	1	1	1
Long-grain rice	100 g	4 oz	½ cup
Chicken stock	450 ml	¾ pt	2 cups
Chopped fresh parsley	30 ml	2 tbsp	2 tbsp
Salt and freshly ground black pepper			

method

1. Place the butter or margarine in a large bowl and microwave on High for 45 seconds until melted. Stir in the onion and garlic and microwave on High for 1-2 minutes until just softened.

2. Stir in the rice until well coated in butter or margarine. Stir in the stock and parsley and season with salt and pepper. Cover and microwave on High for 4 minutes then on Medium for 12-15 minutes until the rice is tender and the stock has been absorbed, stirring once or twice during cooking.

3. Leave to stand, covered, for 4 minutes then stir well before serving.

TOMATO RICE SPECIAL

ingredients	Metric	Imperial	American
Butter or margarine	25 g	1 oz	2 tbsp
Onion, finely chopped	1	1	1
Garlic clove, crushed	1	1	1
Celery stalk, chopped	1	1	1
Carrot, chopped	1	1	1
Long-grain rice	100 g	4 oz	½ cup
Canned tomatoes, chopped	400 g	14 oz	14 oz
Tomato purée (paste)	15 ml	1 tbsp	1 tbsp
Dried oregano	5 ml	1 tsp	1 tsp
Chicken stock	375 ml	13 fl oz	1½ cups
Cooked peeled prawns (shrimps)	100 g	4 oz	¼ lb

method

1. Place the butter or margarine in a bowl and microwave on High for 45 seconds until melted. Stir in the onion, garlic, celery and carrot and microwave on High for 3 minutes.

2. Stir in the rice until the grains are coated in fat. Stir in all the remaining ingredients except the prawns. Cover and microwave on High for 5 minutes then on Medium for 12-15 minutes until the rice is tender and the stock has been absorbed, stirring once or twice during cooking.

3. Stir in the prawns, cover and microwave on Medium for 45 seconds. Leave to stand, covered, for 5 minutes before serving.

KEDGEREE

ingredients	Metric	Imperial	American
Butter or margarine	25 g	1 oz	2 tbsp
Onion, sliced	1	1	1
Garlic clove, chopped	1	1	1
Red pepper, chopped	1	1	1
Long-grain rice	175 g	6 oz	¾ cup
Hot vegetable stock	300 ml	½ pt	1¼ cups
Boiling water	300 ml	½ pt	1¼ cups
Salt and freshly ground black pepper			
Smoked haddock, skinned and flaked	225 g	8 oz	½ lb
Hard-boiled (hard-cooked) eggs, quartered	2	2	2

method

1. Place the butter or margarine, onion and garlic in a casserole dish and microwave on High for 2-3 minutes until just soft.

2. Stir in the pepper, rice, stock and water and season with salt and pepper. Cover and microwave on High for 15 minutes until the rice is almost tender, stirring twice during cooking. Add a little more liquid if the mixture becomes too dry.

3. Stir in the haddock and eggs, cover and microwave for a further 5 minutes.

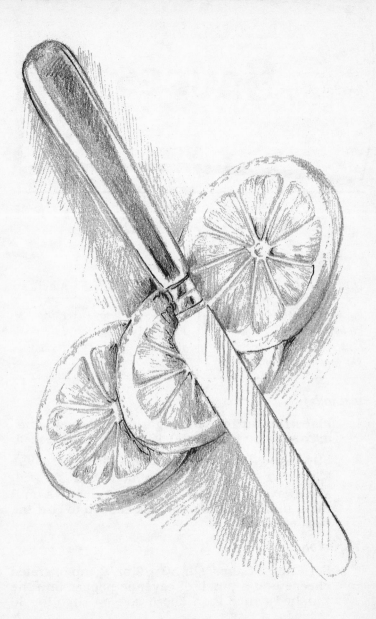

SAUCES

WHITE SAUCE

ingredients	Metric	Imperial	American
Butter or margarine	15 ml	1 tbsp	1 tbsp
Plain (all-purpose) flour	15 ml	1 tbsp	1 tbsp
Milk	300 ml	½ pt	1¼ cups
Salt and black pepper			

method

1. Place the butter or margarine in a bowl and microwave on High for 30-40 seconds until melted.

2. Stir in the flour then gradually stir in the milk. Microwave on High for 1-1½ minutes then stir well. Microwave on High for a further 1½ minutes until the sauce is smooth and thick enough to coat the back of a spoon.

Variations

For Cheese Sauce, stir 50 g/2 oz/½ cup of grated cheese and a pinch of cayenne pepper into the finished sauce then microwave on High for 30 seconds.

For Herb Sauce, stir 30-45 ml/2-3 tbsp of chopped fresh herbs of your choice into the finished sauce.

For Mushroom Sauce, add 50 g/2 oz sliced mushrooms and 5 ml/1 tsp of lemon juice to the melted butter or margarine then continue as before.

For Onion Sauce, add 1 finely sliced onion to the butter or margarine and microwave on High for 2 minutes then continue as before.

For Parsley Sauce, stir 5 ml/1 tsp of lemon juice and 30 ml/2tbsp of chopped fresh parsley into the finished sauce.

For Prawn Sauce, stir 50 g/2 oz of cooked peeled prawns, 30 ml/2tbsp of double (heavy) cream and 2.5 ml/½ tsp of lemon juice into the cooked sauce and microwave on High for 1 minute.

BEARNAISE SAUCE

ingredients	Metric	Imperial	American
Egg yolks	3	3	3
White wine vinegar	10 ml	2 tsp	2 tsp
Chopped fresh tarragon	5 ml	1 tsp	1 tsp
Salt and freshly ground black pepper			
Butter or margarine	100 g	4 oz	½ cup
Grated onion	1	1	1

method

1. Put the egg yolks, wine vinegar and tarragon in a food processor or blender and season with salt and pepper. Process for a few seconds until smooth.

2. Put the butter or margarine and onion into a small bowl and microwave on High for 45 seconds until the butter has melted.

3. With the motor running, gradually add the butter mixture to the egg yolk mixture through the feed tube in a slow, steady stream. The sauce will slowly thicken as the butter is absorbed. Serve immediately.

HOLLANDAISE SAUCE

ingredients	Metric	Imperial	American
White wine vinegar	30 ml	2 tbsp	2 tbsp
Egg yolks	3	3	3
Unsalted butter, diced	100 g	4 oz	½ cup
Pinch of salt			

method

1. Put the wine vinegar and egg yolks in a bowl and mix well. Add the butter and microwave on High for 1 minute, whisking every 5-10 seconds during cooking.

2. Season to taste with salt.

BREAD SAUCE

ingredients	Metric	Imperial	American
Small onion	1	1	1
Peppercorns	5	5	5
Pinch of grated nutmeg			
Small bay leaf	1	1	1
Milk	300 ml	½ pt	1¼ cups
Breadcrumbs	50 g	2 oz	½ cup
Butter or margarine	25 g	1 oz	2 tbsp
Salt and freshly ground black pepper			

method

1. Put the onion, peppercorns, nutmeg, bay leaf and milk in a bowl and microwave on High for 2 minutes. Leave to stand for 5 minutes.

2. Strain the flavoured milk over the breadcrumbs and butter. Mix well. Microwave on High for 2 minutes then stir well and season to taste with salt and pepper.

APPLE SAUCE

ingredients	Metric	Imperial	American
Cooking apples, peeled, cored and sliced	450 g	1 lb	1 lb
Pinch of salt			
Sugar	15 ml	1 tbsp	1 tbsp
Butter or margarine	15 ml	1 tbsp	1 tbsp

method

1. Place the apples in a bowl, cover and microwave on High for 5-6 minutes until soft.

2. Purée the apples in a food processor or blender or rub them through a sieve.

3. Return the apple purée to the bowl and stir in the salt, sugar and butter. Microwave on High for 1 minute.

TARTARE SAUCE

ingredients	Metric	Imperial	American
Small onion, chopped	1	1	1
Oil	5 ml	1 tsp	1 tsp
Chopped fresh chives	5 ml	1 tsp	1 tsp
Salt and freshly ground black pepper			
Mayonnaise	150 ml	¼ pt	⅔ cup
Finely chopped gherkins	30 ml	2 tbsp	2 tbsp
Lemon juice	5 ml	1 tsp	1 tsp

method

1. Place the onion, oil and chives in a small bowl and season with salt and pepper. Cover and microwave on High for 1-2 minutes until the onion is just tender. Leave to cool slightly.

2. Blend in the remaining ingredients, cover and chill for at least 1 hour before serving.

TOMATO SAUCE

ingredients	Metric	Imperial	American
Butter or margarine	25 g	1 oz	2 tbsp
Red pepper, chopped	1	1	1
Small onion, chopped	1	1	1
Canned chopped tomatoes	400 g	14 oz	14 oz
Tomato purée (paste)	60 ml	4 tbsp	4 tbsp
Soft brown sugar	15 ml	1 tbsp	1 tbsp
Dried oregano	5 ml	1 tsp	1 tsp

method

1. Place the butter, pepper and onion in a bowl. Cover and microwave on High for 2 minutes, stirring once during cooking.

2. Add the tomatoes, tomato purée, sugar and oregano and microwave, uncovered, on High for 3-4 minutes until cooked through and blended, stirring once or twice during cooking.

3. Purée the sauce in a food processor or blender.

CHOCOLATE SAUCE

ingredients	Metric	Imperial	American
Chocolate	100 g	4 oz	¼ lb
Butter	15 ml	1 tbsp	1 tbsp
Water	30 ml	2 tbsp	2 tbsp
Golden (light corn) syrup	30 ml	2 tbsp	2 tbsp

method

1. Place all the ingredients in a bowl and microwave on High for 2-3 minutes until blended, stirring once or twice during cooking. The sauce will thicken as it cools slightly.

CRANBERRY SAUCE

ingredients	Metric	Imperial	American
Cranberries	225 g	8 oz	½ lb
Water	150 ml	¼ pt	⅔ cup
Granulated sugar	175 g	6 oz	¾ cup
Lemon juice	10 ml	2 tsp	2 tsp
Grated rind of lemon	½	½	½

method

1. Place all the ingredients in a bowl. Cover and microwave on High for 5-6 minutes, stirring vigorously twice during cooking.

2. Microwave on Low for a further 7-8 minutes, stirring regularly during cooking.

3. Leave to cool, covered, before serving.

CUSTARD

ingredients	Metric	Imperial	American
Milk	300 ml	½ pt	1¼ cups
Egg yolks	2	2	2
Caster (superfine) sugar	25 g	1 oz	2 tbsp
Few drops of vanilla essence (extract)			

method

1. Place the milk, egg yolks and sugar in a large bowl and microwave on High for 3-4 minutes until the custard is thick enough to coat the back of a wooden spoon, whisking 4 times during cooking. Do not allow the custard to boil otherwise the eggs will curdle.

2. Stir in the vanilla essence and serve.

MARSHMALLOW SAUCE

ingredients	Metric	Imperial	American
Marshmallows	100 g	4 oz	¼ lb
Evaporated milk	30 ml	2 tbsp	2 tbsp
Strong black coffee	30 ml	2 tbsp	2 tbsp

method

1. Place all the ingredients in a bowl and microwave on Medium for 1-2 minutes until blended, stirring once or twice during cooking.

ORANGE SAUCE

ingredients	Metric	Imperial	American
Cornflour (cornstarch)	10 ml	2 tsp	2 tsp
Caster (superfine) sugar	100 g	4 oz	½ cup
Unsalted butter	50 g	2 oz	¼ cup
Grated rind and juice of orange	1	1	1
Water	300 ml	½ pt	1¼ cups

method

1. Place all the ingredients in a bowl and microwave on High for 3-4 minutes until well blended, whisking once or twice during cooking.

Variation

For a Lemon Sauce, substitute lemon rind and juice for the orange.

STRAWBERRY JAM SAUCE

ingredients	Metric	Imperial	American
Strawberry jam	100 g	4 oz	¼ lb
Lemon juice	5 ml	1 tsp	1 tsp
Water	30 ml	2 tbsp	2 tbsp

method

1. Place all the ingredients in a bowl and microwave on High for 20 seconds until blended, stirring once or twice during cooking.

DESSERTS

APPLE CRUMBLE PIE

ingredients	Metric	Imperial	American
Eating apples, peeled, cored and grated	450 g	1 lb	1 lb
Lemon juice	30 ml	2 tbsp	2 tbsp
Sugar	75 g	3 oz	1/3 cup
Ground cinnamon	5 ml	1 tsp	1 tsp
Cooked 23 cm/9 in shortcrust pastry case (see page 152)	1	1	1
Butter or margarine	40 g	1½ oz	3 tbsp
Plain (all-purpose) flour	75 g	3 oz	¾ cup
Soft brown sugar	75 g	3 oz	1/3 cup
Mixed spice	2.5 ml	½ tsp	½ tsp
Pinch of salt			

method

1. Toss the eating apples in the lemon juice. Stir in the sugar and cinnamon and spoon into the prepared pastry case.

2. Microwave on Medium for 15-20 minutes until the apples are slightly soft and the centre is hot.

3. Meanwhile, rub the butter or margarine into the flour then stir in the sugar, spice and salt.

Sprinkle over the apples and microwave on High for 4-5 minutes.

Variation

You can bake the apple crumble without the pastry shell if you prefer, or use other fruits instead of the apples.

▼

BREAD AND BUTTER PUDDING

ingredients	Metric	Imperial	American
Bread slices, crusts removed	8	8	8
Butter or margarine	50 g	2 oz	¼ cup
Sultanas (golden raisins)	50 g	2 oz	⅓ cup
Caster (superfine) sugar	45 ml	3 tbsp	3 tbsp
Milk	600 ml	1 pt	2½ cups
Eggs, beaten	2	2	2
Grated nutmeg			

method

1. Spread the bread with the butter or margarine and arrange the slices in a buttered casserole dish, layering them with the sultanas and sugar.

2. Place the milk in a bowl and microwave on High for 2 minutes until warm. Beat in the eggs then pour the mixture over the bread and leave to stand for 5 minutes. Sprinkle with nutmeg.

3. Microwave on Low for 12-15 minutes until just set.

CREME CARAMEL

ingredients	Metric	Imperial	American
Caster (superfine) sugar	45 ml	3 tbsp	3 tbsp
Water	60 ml	4 tbsp	4 tbsp
Milk	300 ml	½ pt	1¼ cups
Eggs, beaten	2	2	2

method

1. Mix 30 ml/2 tbsp of sugar with the water in a Pyrex casserole dish and microwave on High for 4 minutes, stirring well half way through cooking.

2. Place the milk and remaining sugar in a glass bowl and microwave on High for 2 minutes until the sugar has dissolved, stirring once during cooking.

3. Beat in the eggs when pour through a sieve on to the caramel. Cover and microwave on Low for 8-10 minutes until almost set.

4. Leave to cool before turning out to serve.

DRIED FRUIT COMPOTE

ingredients	Metric	Imperial	American
Prunes, stoned	225 g	8 oz	½ lb
Dried apricots	225 g	8 oz	½ lb
Dried apple rings	100 g	4 oz	¼ lb
Sultanas (golden raisins)	50 g	2 oz	⅓ cup
Chopped mixed nuts	15 ml	1 tbsp	1 tbsp
Honey	30 ml	2 tbsp	2 tbsp
Dry white wine	120 ml	4 fl oz	½ cup

method

1. Soak the prunes in boiling water for 1 hour then drain.

2. Mix together all the ingredients and microwave on High for 10 minutes.

3. Leave to cool then serve with cream.

SPICED PEARS IN WINE

ingredients	Metric	Imperial	American
Caster (superfine) sugar	100 g	4 oz	½ cup
Red wine	300 ml	½ pt	1¼ cups
Lemon juice	5 ml	1 tsp	1 tsp
Cinnamon stick	1	1	1
Cloves	4	4	4
Pears, peeled and cored	4	4	4

method

1. Place the sugar, wine, lemon juice, cinnamon and cloves in a bowl and microwave on High for 4-5 minutes until boiling, stirring 4 or 5 times during cooking to make sure that the sugar has dissolved. Leave to stand for 10 minutes.

2. Strain the syrup into a deep bowl and add the pears, coating them well with the syrup. Cover and microwave on High for 5-7 minutes, spooning the juice over the pears once or twice during cooking.

3. Leave to cool then serve with cream.

ICE CREAM

ingredients	Metric	Imperial	American
Milk	300 ml	½ pt	1¼ cups
Caster (superfine) sugar	100 g	4 oz	½ cup
Eggs, beaten	2	2	2
Vanilla essence (extract)	5 ml	1 tsp	1 tsp
Double (heavy) cream, whipped	300 ml	½ pt	1¼ cups

method

1. Place the milk and sugar in a bowl and microwave on High for 2-3 minutes until the sugar is dissolved and the milk is warm, stirring once or twice during cooking.

2. Whisk in the eggs and vanilla essence and microwave on High for 2-3 minutes until thick and smooth, stirring once or twice during cooking.

3. Leave to cool then fold in the cream. Pour into a freezer container and leave until beginning to freeze around the edge.

4. Whisk again, then return to the freezer to set.

Variations

For Chocolate Chip Ice Cream, add 100 g/4 oz/ ¼ lb chocolate chips with the cream.

For Coffee Ice Cream, replace the vanilla essence with coffee essence.

For Strawberry Ripple Ice Cream, swirl in 1 quantity of Strawberry Jam Sauce (see page 122) after you have folded in the cream.

CHRISTMAS PUDDING

ingredients	Metric	Imperial	American
White breadcrumbs	75 g	3 oz	3 slices
Plain (all-purpose) flour	50 g	2 oz	½ cup
Bicarbonate of soda (baking soda)	5 ml	1 tsp	1 tsp
Mixed spice	5 ml	1 tsp	1 tsp
Pinch of grated nutmeg			
Pinch of salt			
Currants	50 g	2 oz	⅓ cup
Raisins	100 g	4 oz	⅔ cup
Sultanas (golden raisins)	50 g	2 oz	⅓ cup
Soft brown sugar	50 g	2 oz	¼ cup
Butter or margarine, softened	50 g	2 oz	¼ cup
Milk	120 ml	4 fl oz	½ cup
Golden (light corn) syrup	30 ml	2 tbsp	2 tbsp
Egg, beaten	1	1	1
Sherry	45 ml	3 tbsp	3 tbsp
Brandy	30 ml	2 tbsp	2 tbsp

method

1. Mix together the breadcrumbs, flour, bicarbonate of soda, spices and salt. Stir in the fruit and sugar.

2. Beat in the butter or margarine, milk, syrup, egg and sherry until the mixture is well blended.

3. Grease a large pudding basin. Cut 2 strips of greaseproof paper and lay them in the basin in a cross so that they overhang the sides.

   . Spoon the mixture into the basin, cover and microwave on Medium for 8-12 minutes until springy to the touch, checking every 2 minutes.

5. Leave to stand, covered, for 5 minutes then turn out on to a serving plate, using the greaseproof strips to help.

6. Pour the brandy into a bowl and microwave on High for 20 seconds until warm. Pour over the pudding and ignite it to serve.

LEMON LAYER SPONGE

ingredients	Metric	Imperial	American
Grated rind and juice of lemon	1	1	1
Butter or margarine	50 g	2 oz	¼ cup
Caster (superfine) sugar	100 g	4 oz	½ cup
Eggs, separated	2	2	2
Self-raising flour	50 g	2 oz	½ cup
Milk	300 ml	½ pt	1¼ cups

method

1. Place the lemon rind, butter or margarine and sugar in a bowl and beat until light and fluffy. Add the egg yolks and flour and beat well. Stir in the milk and 45 ml/3 tbsp of lemon juice.

2. Whisk the egg whites until stiff then fold them into the sponge mixture. Pour the mixture into an 18 cm/7 in soufflé dish and microwave on Medium for 4-5 minutes until the top is just set and the base has become a lemon custard sauce.

RICE PUDDING

ingredients	Metric	Imperial	American
Short-grain rice	50 g	2 oz	¼ cup
Milk	600 ml	1 pt	2½ cups
Sugar	25 g	1 oz	2 tbsp
Butter or margarine	25 g	1 oz	2 tbsp
Sultanas (golden raisins)	50 g	2 oz	⅓ cup
Pinch of grated nutmeg			

method

1. Stir the rice, milk and sugar together in a large casserole dish and dot with the butter. Cover and microwave on Low for 20 minutes, stirring twice during cooking.

2. Add the sultanas and microwave on Low for a further 10 minutes.

3. Sprinkle with nutmeg and leave to stand for 10 minutes. If the pudding is too runny, microwave on Low for a further 5 minutes.

PINEAPPLE UPSIDE-DOWN

ingredients	Metric	Imperial	American
For the topping:			
Butter or margarine	25 g	1 oz	2 tbsp
Golden (light corn) syrup	30 ml	2 tbsp	2 tbsp
Canned pineapple rings, drained	350 g	12 oz	¾ lb
For the sponge:			
Butter or margarine	175 g	6 oz	¾ cup
Soft brown sugar	175 g	6 oz	¾ cup
Eggs, beaten	3	3	3
Plain (all-purpose) flour	175 g	6 oz	1½ cups
Baking powder	15 ml	1 tbsp	1 tbsp
Vanilla essence (extract)	5 ml	1 tsp	1 tsp

method

1. Place the butter or margarine and syrup for the topping in the base of a large shallow dish and microwave on High for 25 seconds. Mix together then arrange the pineapple rings on the topping.

2. Cream the butter and sugar until soft then beat in the eggs, flour, baking powder and vanilla essence. Pour the mixture over the pineapple and smooth the top. Microwave on High for 12-15 minutes until just set.

3. Leave to stand for 5 minutes then turn out and serve hot or cold with cream.

STRAWBERRY MILLE FEUILLES

ingredients	Metric	Imperial	American
Frozen puff pastry, thawed	450 g	1 lb	1 lb
Strawberries, halved	350 g	12 oz	¾ lb
Double (heavy) cream, whipped	300 ml	½ pt	1¼ cups
Strawberry jam	30 ml	2 tbsp	2 tbsp
Water	15 ml	1 tbsp	1 tbsp

method

1. Divide the pastry into thirds and roll out each piece to a 20 x 10 cm/8 x 4 in rectangle. Prick with a fork.

2. Microwave each piece of pastry separately on a sheet of greaseproof paper on High for 3 minutes until crisp. Leave to cool then trim to the same size.

3. Reserve one-third of the strawberry halves and chop the remainder. Mix the chopped strawberries with the cream.

4. Place a slice of pastry on a plate and cover with half the strawberry and cream mixture. Top with a second pastry slice and cover with the remaining strawberries and cream. Cover with the final slice and arrange and strawberry halves on top.

5. Put the jam and water in a small bowl and microwave on High for 1 minute. Brush over the strawberries then cool and chill before serving.

Cakes, Biscuits and Sweets

APPLE CAKE

ingredients	Metric	Imperial	American
Plain (all-purpose) flour	75 g	3 oz	¾ cup
Soft brown sugar	100 g	4 oz	½ cup
Bicarbonate of soda (baking soda)	5 ml	1 tsp	1 tsp
Mixed spice	2.5 ml	½ tsp	½ tsp
Pinch of salt			
Butter or margarine, softened	75 g	3 oz	⅓ cup
Vanilla essence (extract)	5 ml	1 tsp	1 tsp
Apples, peeled, cored and chopped	450 g	1 lb	1 lb
Chopped mixed nuts	75 g	3 oz	¾ cup
Icing (confectioners') sugar	75 g	3 oz	⅓ cup
Milk	5-10 ml	1-2 tsp	1-2 tsp

method

1. Mix together the flour, sugar, bicarbonate of soda, spice, salt, butter or margarine and vanilla essence. Stir in the apples and nuts.

2. Spread the mixture in a lined 23 cm/9 in cake dish and level the top. Microwave on Medium for 5 minutes. Microwave on High for 3-5 minutes until springy to touch.

3. Leave to stand for 5 minutes then turn out on to a wire rack to cool.

4. Sieve the icing sugar into a small bowl and add the milk a little at a time until just blended. Spoon the icing over the cake.

OATCAKES

ingredients	Metric	Imperial	American
Wholemeal flour	*100g*	*4 oz*	*1 cup*
Rolled oats	*50g*	*2 oz*	*½ cup*
Light brown sugar	*30 ml*	*2 tbsp*	*2 tbsp*
Pinch of salt			
Vegetable fat	*50 g*	*2 oz*	*¼ cup*
Egg, beaten	*1*	*1*	*1*

method

1. Mix together the flour, oats, sugar and salt. Rub in the fat the blend in the egg to make a dough.

2. Roll out to 5 mm/¼ in thick and cut into rounds. Arrange on greased greaseproof paper and microwave on High for 3 minutes, rearranging once during cooking.

ALL-IN-ONE SPONGE CAKE

ingredients	Metric	Imperial	American
Self-raising flour	150 g	6 oz	1½ cups
Soft margarine	100 g	4 oz	½ cup
Caster (superfine) sugar	100 g	4 oz	½ cup
Eggs	2	2	2
Milk	45 ml	3 tbsp	3 tbsp
For the icing:			
Icing (confectioners') sugar	100 g	4 oz	½ cup
Butter or margarine	50 g	2 oz	¼ cup

method

1. Mix together all the cake ingredients until smooth.

2. Line the base of a 18 cm/7 in soufflé dish with greaseproof paper then pour in the cake mixture. Smooth the top. Microwave on Medium for 5-6 minutes until cooked.

3. Leave to cool slightly in the dish before turning out to cool completely.

4. To make the icing, beat the butter or margarine until light and fluffy then beat in the sugar. Beat in the chosen flavouring, if using, before icing the cake.

Variations

For Chocolate Cake, replace 50 g/2 oz/¼ cup of the flour with cocoa powder (unsweetened chocolate). Flavour the icing with 15ml/1 tbsp of cocoa powder (unsweetened chocolate).

For Chocolate Chip Cake, add 100 g/4 oz/1 cup of chocolate chips to the mixture. Flavour the icing with 15 ml/1 tbsp of cocoa powder (unsweetened chocolate).

For Marble Cake, divide the mixture into 3 and colour each one with a few drops of different food colourings. Spoon alternate colours into the dish and swirl them lightly together before baking.

For Orange Cake, add the grated rind and juice of 1 orange instead of the milk. Flavour the icing with the grated rind of an orange and 5 ml/ 1 teaspoon of the juice.

FLAPJACKS

ingredients	Metric	Imperial	American
Butter or magarine	100g	4 oz	½ cup
Caster sugar	25 g	1 oz	2 tbsp
Soft brown sugar	50 g	2 oz	¼ cup
Golden (corn) syrup	30 ml	2 tbsp	2 tbsp
Pinch of salt			
Rolled oats	200 g	7 oz	1¾ cups

method

1. Place the butter or magarine and sugars in a bowl and microwave on High for 1 ½ minutes.

2. Blend in the remaining ingredients and press into a greased 23 cm/9 in square dish. Microwave on High for 5 minutes.

CHOCOLATE BROWNIES

ingredients	Metric	Imperial	American
Cocoa powder (unsweetened chocolate)	30 ml	2 tbsp	2 tbsp
Water	120 ml	4 fl oz	½ cup
Oil	45 ml	3 tbsp	3 tbsp
Plain (all-purpose) flour	100 g	4 oz	1 cup
Granulated sugar	225 g	8 oz	1 cup
Pinch of salt			
Bicarbonate of soda (baking soda)	2.5 ml	½ tsp	½ tsp
Ground cinnamon	2.5 ml	½ tsp	½ tsp
Egg, beaten	1	1	1
Milk	45 ml	3 tbsp	3 tbsp
Few drops of vanilla essence (extract)			
For the topping:			
Butter or margarine	50 g	2 oz	¼ cup
Milk	45 ml	3 tbsp	3 tbsp
Cocoa powder (unsweetened chocolate)	30 ml	2 tbsp	2 tbsp
Icing (confectioners') sugar	175 g	6 oz	¾ cup

method

1. Blend together the cocoa and water in a small bowl then stir in the oil. Microwave on High for 3 minutes until boiling.

2. Mix together the flour, sugar, salt, bicarbonate of soda and cinnamon. Stir in the hot cocoa mixture and beat until thoroughly blended. Stir in the egg, milk and vanilla essence and beat well.

3. Pour into a 23 cm/9 in square baking dish and cover the corners with foil. Microwave on Medium

140

for 6-7 minutes. Remove the foil and microwave on Medium for 4-5 minutes until the centre is springy when touched. Leave to stand for 5 minutes.

4. To make the icing, mix together the butter, milk and cocoa and microwave on High for 2-3 minutes until boiling, stirring twice during cooking. Beat in the icing sugar until smooth. Spread the mixture over the top of the cake and leave to set.

5. Cut into squares when cool.

ICED CARROT CAKE

ingredients	Metric	Imperial	American
Self-raising flour	225 g	8 oz	2 cups
Baking powder	10 ml	2 tsp	2 tsp
Salt	5 ml	1 tsp	1 tsp
Soft brown sugar	150 g	5 oz	2/3 cup
Oil	150 ml	1/4 pt	3/4 cup
Eggs	3	3	3
Carrots, grated	225 g	8 oz	1/2 lb
Walnuts, finely chopped	50 g	2 oz	1/2 cup
For the icing:			
Cream cheese	100 g	4 oz	1/2 cup
Icing (confectioners') sugar	50 g	2 oz	1/4 cup
Lemon juice	30 ml	2 tbsp	2 tbsp

method

1. Line a 20 cm/8 in soufflé dish with greaseproof paper.

2. Mix together the flour, baking powder, salt and sugar.

3. Beat together the oil and eggs then stir it into the dry ingredients with the carrots and walnuts.

4. Pour into the soufflé dish and microwave on Medium for 8-10 minutes until firm. Leave to cool slightly in the dish before turning out to cool completely on a wire rack.

5. Beat together the icing ingredients until smooth then use to ice the cake.

FRUIT CAKE

ingredients	Metric	Imperial	American
Soft margarine	100 g	4 oz	½ cup
Self-raising flour	225 g	8 oz	2 cups
Soft brown sugar	100 g	4 oz	½ cup
Sultanas (golden raisins)	175 g	6 oz	1 cup
Eggs	2	2	2
Golden (light corn) syrup	15 ml	1 tbsp	1 tbsp
Milk	30 ml	2 tbsp	2 tbsp
Glacé cherries, halved	50 g	2 oz	¼ cup
Walnut halves	8	8	8
Apricot jam, sieved	30 ml	2 tbsp	2 tbsp
Water	15 ml	1 tbsp	1 tbsp

method

1. Line the base of an 18 cm/7 in soufflé dish with greaseproof paper.

2. Rub the margarine into the flour until the mixture resembles breadcrumbs. Stir in the sugar and sultanas and make a well in the centre of the mixture.

3. Beat together the eggs, syrup and milk. Stir into the dry ingredients until well blended.

4. Pour into the soufflé dish and microwave on Medium for 5-6 minutes. Turn out on to a wire rack to cool.

5. Decorate the top with glacé cherries and walnuts halves. Microwave the apricot jam and water in a bowl on High for 1 minute then brush over the fruit and nuts to glaze.

FRESH FRUIT CHEESECAKE

ingredients	Metric	Imperial	American
Butter or margarine	50 g	2 oz	¼ cup
Digestive biscuits (Graham crackers), crushed	100 g	4 oz	1 cup
Curd cheese	225 g	8 oz	1 cup
2 eggs, separated			
Caster (superfine) sugar	50 g	2 oz	¼ cup
Gelatine	15 g	½ oz	1 sachet
Water	75 ml	5 tbsp	5 tbsp
Double (heavy) cream, whipped	150 ml	¼ pt	⅔ cup
Fresh fruit, sliced	450 g	1 lb	1 lb

method

1. Put the butter or margarine in a bowl and microwave on High for 45 seconds until melted. Stir in the biscuit crumbs.

2. Press the mixture evenly over the bottom of a greased loose-bottomed 20 cm/8 in round cake dish and chill.

3. Beat the cheese, egg yolks and sugar.

4. Put the gelatine and water in a bowl and microwave on High for 30 seconds until the gelatine has dissolved. Stir well and leave to cool slightly then beat into the cheese mixture. Leave to one side until beginning to set.

5. Whisk the egg whites until stiff. Fold them into the cheese mixture then fold in the whipped cream. Spoon over the base and smooth the top. Chill until set.

6. Decorate the top with fresh fruit of your choice.

GINGERBREAD

ingredients	Metric	Imperial	American
Plain (all-purpose) flour	75 g	3 oz	¾ cup
Wholemeal flour	50 g	2 oz	½ cup
Bicarbonate of soda (baking soda)	5 ml	1 tsp	1 tsp
Butter or margarine, softened	100 g	4 oz	½ cup
Soft brown sugar	75 g	3 oz	⅓ cup
Black treacle	100 g	4 oz	⅓ cup
Orange juice	75 ml	5 tbsp	5 tbsp
Grated orange rind	5 ml	1 tsp	1 tsp
Ground cinnamon	5 ml	1 tsp	1 tsp
Ground ginger	2.5 ml	½ tsp	½ tsp
Eggs, beaten	2	2	2

method

1. Mix together all the ingredients until thoroughly blended. Pour the mixture into a 23 cm/9 in cake dish and microwave on Medium for 6 minutes. Microwave on High for 3-6 minutes until the centre is just springy.

2. Leave to stand for 10 minutes before turning out and leaving to cool.

BANANA NUT BREAD

ingredients	Metric	Imperial	American
Wholemeal flour	100 g	4 oz	1 cup
Plain (all-purpose) flour	50 g	2 oz	½ cup
Soft brown sugar	175 g	6 oz	⅔ cup
Butter or margarine, softened	100 g	4 oz	½ cup
Milk	75 ml	5 tbsp	5 tbsp
Eggs, beaten	2	2	2
Bananas, mashed	2	2	2
Chopped walnuts	25 g	1 oz	¼ cup
Bicarbonate of soda (baking soda)	5 ml	1 tsp	1 tsp
Ground cinnamon	5 ml	1 tsp	1 tsp

method

1. Mix together all the ingredients and beat until well blended. Turn into a lined 900 g/2 lb loaf dish and shield the ends with strips of foil.

2. Microwave on Medium for 7-8 minutes, then microwave on High for 3 minutes. Remove the foil and microwave on High for 3-5 minutes until the centre is springy.

3. Leave to stand for 5 minutes before turning out.

OAT AND COCONUT BARS

ingredients	Metric	Imperial	American
Demerara sugar	100 g	4 oz	½ cup
Rolled oats	100 g	4 oz	¼ lb
Desiccated coconut	25 g	1 oz	¼ cup
Soft margarine	100 g	4 oz	½ cup

method

1. Mix together the sugar, oats and coconut in a bowl. Beat in the margarine.

2. Line a square dish with greaseproof paper and press the mixture into the dish. Microwave on High for 4-5 minutes.

3. Cut into about 15 squares while still hot.

CHOCOLATE FUDGE

ingredients	Metric	Imperial	American
Caster (superfine) sugar	450 g	1 lb	2 cups
Water	60 ml	4 tbsp	4 tbsp
Condensed milk	150 ml	¼ pt	⅔ cup
Plain (semi-sweet) chocolate	100 g	4 oz	¼ lb

method

1. Place all the ingredients in a large bowl. Cook on High for 4-5 minutes until the chocolate has melted and the sugar has completely dissolved, stirring occasionally during cooking. Microwave on Medium for an extra 2-3 minutes if they have not dissolved.

2. Microwave on High for 5 minutes then stir well. Microwave for a further 5 minutes and stir, then 5 minutes again and stir until the mixture is thick and a drop in cold water forms a soft ball when rolled between finger and thumb.

3. Leave the mixture to cool.

4. Beat the fudge with a wooden spoon until it is very thick and creamy. Pour into a lightly greased square dish and cut into about 40 squares when cold.

COCONUT ICE

ingredients	Metric	Imperial	American
Granulated sugar	450 g	1 lb	2 cups
Milk	150 ml	¼ pt	⅔ cup
Desiccated coconut	150 g	5 oz	1¼ cups
Red food colouring (optional)			

method

1. Place the sugar and milk in a large bowl and microwave on High for 5 minutes until the sugar has completely dissolved, stirring occasionally during cooking.

2. Stir in the coconut and microwave on High for 8-10 minutes until the mixture is thick and a drop in cold water forms a soft ball when rolled between finger and thumb. Pour half the mixture into a greased baking tray.

3. Stir a few drops of food colouring, if using, into the remaining mixture then pour it over the first layer. Leave until half set then mark into squares. Leave until set before cutting into about 36 squares.

PASTRY AND PRESERVES

SHORTCRUST PASTRY FLAN CASE

ingredients	Metric	Imperial	American
Plain (all-purpose) flour	100 g	4 oz	1 cup
Salt	2.5 ml	½ tsp	½ tsp
Lard or vegetable fat	25 g	1 oz	1 oz
Butter or margarine	25 g	1 oz	1 oz
Cold water	30-60 ml	2-4 tbsp	2-4 tbsp

method

1. Mix the flour and salt in a bowl. Rub in the lard and butter or margarine until the mixture resembles breadcrumbs. Gradually mix in the water until the mixture binds together to a pastry.

2. Shape the pastry into a ball then roll out on a lightly floured surface to a 28 cm/11 in circle. Lift the pastry on to a 23 cm/9 in flan ring and trim and shape the edges. Prick the base with a fork.

3. Microwave on High for 5-7 minutes until the pastry is dry and opaque. Leave to cool before filling.

BISCUIT CRUMB FLAN RING

ingredients	Metric	Imperial	American
Butter or margarine	50 g	2 oz	¼ cup
Digestive biscuits (Graham crackers), crushed	12	12	12
Caster (superfine) sugar	25 g	1 oz	2 tbsp

method

1. Put the butter into a 20 cm/8 in flan dish and microwave on High for 1 minute until melted.

2. Mix together the biscuit crumbs and sugar and sprinkle over the flan dish. Press over the sides and base of the flan to form a shell.

3. Leave to cool and refrigerate before filling.

BLACKBERRY JAM

ingredients	Metric	Imperial	American
Blackberries	*450 g*	*1 lb*	*1 lb*
Caster (superfine) sugar	*450 g*	*1 lb*	*2 cups*
Lemon juice	*30 ml*	*2 tbsp*	*2 tbsp*
Butter or margarine	*5 ml*	*1 tsp*	*1 tsp*

method

1. Place all the ingredients in a large bowl and microwave on High for 5 minutes, stirring occasionally during cooking, until the sugar has melted.

2. Stir all the ingredients together well, making sure the sugar has melted.

3. Microwave on High until setting point is reached. Check after 4 minutes. A spoonful of jam dropped on to a cold saucer will wrinkle when pressed.

4. Leave to cool slightly then stir and pour into 2 x 450 g/1 lb warm jars, seal and label.

LEMON CURD

ingredients	Metric	Imperial	American
Grated rind and juice of lemons	4	4	4
Caster (superfine) sugar	450 g	1 lb	2 cups
Eggs, beaten	4	4	4
Butter or margarine	100 g	4 oz	4 oz

method

1. Place all the ingredients in a large bowl and mix well.

2. Microwave on High for 1 minute then stir well. Continue to cook in 1 minute bursts until the mixture begins to thicken then cook in 30 second bursts until the mixture coats the back of a spoon.

3. Spoon into a warm 450 g/1 lb jar, cover, seal and label.

Variation

For Orange Curd, substitute orange rind and juice for the lemon.

MIXED FRUIT MARMALADE

ingredients	Metric	Imperial	American
Grapefruit	2	2	2
Oranges	2	2	2
Lemons	2	2	2
Water	300 ml	½ pt	1¼ cups
Granulated sugar	900 g	2 lb	4 cups

method

1. Thinly peel the rind from the fruit and cut the rind into shreds. Place in a large bowl with 60 ml/ 4 tbsp of water and microwave on High for 8-10 minutes until soft.

2. Remove and discard the pith from the fruit. Cut the flesh into slices. Tie the pips in a square of muslin.

3. Put the fruit, bag of pips and 300 ml/½ pt/ 1¼ cups of water in a large bowl and microwave on High for 10 minutes. Strain the juice into the rind and stir in the sugar.

4. Microwave on High for 1-2 minutes until the sugar has dissolved then stir well.

5. Microwave on High until setting point is reached. Check after 8 minutes. A spoonful of marmalade dropped on to a cold saucer will wrinkle when pressed.

6. Leave to cool slightly then stir and pour into 2 x 450 g/1 lb warm jars, seal and label.

FRUIT CHUTNEY

ingredients	Metric	Imperial	American
Eating apples, peeled, cored and chopped	3	3	3
Mango, peeled and chopped	1	1	1
Onion, chopped	1	1	1
Soft brown sugar	350 g	12 oz	1½ cups
White wine vinegar	120 ml	4 fl oz	½ cup
Salt	5 ml	1 tsp	1 tsp
Mustard powder	2.5 ml	½ tsp	½ tsp

method

1. Mix together all the ingredients in a large bowl or casserole dish. Microwave on High for 20-25 minutes until soft and thick, stirring twice during cooking.

2. Remove the fruit from the bowl using a slotted spoon and mash it coarsely. Stir it back into the liquid, bottle in 2 x 450 g/1 lb bottles and leave to cool.

3. Store in the refrigerator and use within 2 weeks.

INDEX